William Howard Russell

A Diary in the East

During the Tour of the Prince and Princess of Wales. Vol. 1

William Howard Russell

A Diary in the East
During the Tour of the Prince and Princess of Wales. Vol. 1

ISBN/EAN: 9783337112639

Printed in Europe, USA, Canada, Australia, Japan

Cover: Foto ©ninafisch / pixelio.de

More available books at **www.hansebooks.com**

A
DIARY IN THE EAST.

LONDON :

PRINTED BY WOODFALL AND KINDER,

MILFORD LANE, STRAND, W.C.

SHIPS OF THE DESER

Vincent Brooks Day & Son, London

A

DIARY IN THE EAST

DURING THE TOUR

OF THE

PRINCE AND PRINCESS OF WALES.

BY

WILLIAM HOWARD RUSSELL.

WITH ILLUSTRATIONS.

IN TWO VOLUMES.—VOL. I.

LONDON:

GEORGE ROUTLEDGE AND SONS.
THE BROADWAY, LUDGATE.
1869.

TO HER ROYAL HIGHNESS

THE PRINCESS OF WALES.

———◆———

Madam,

The gracious permission I have received from your Royal Highness to dedicate this Volume to you, causes me to feel regret that it is not more worthy of that great honour; but I trust that the goodness which induced your Royal Highness to confer such a favour on the Work, will lead you to regard with an indulgent eye this Record of the interesting Tour in part of which I accompanied the Prince of Wales.

I am, Madam, with profound respect,

Your Royal Highness's

Most faithful, obliged, and humble Servant,

WILLIAM HOWARD RUSSELL·

TO THE READER.

It will be seen from the concluding paragraph of the Preface, that I intended to include in this work a chapter on the Nile Basin and on the Suez Canal from a scientific point of view, as well as some observations on the Ornithology and Natural History of Egypt, for which I would have been indebted to Professor Owen and others.

The size of the volume has, however, far exceeded my original design, and I am obliged, very unwillingly, to omit the contributions to which the Preface refers.

W. H. RUSSELL.

CONTENTS.

CHAPTER IV.

CHAPTER V.

CHAPTER VI.

CHAPTER VII.

CHAPTER VIII.

CHAPTER IX.

CHAPTER X.

CHAPTER XI.

CHAPTER XII.

CHAPTER XIII.

CHAPTER XIV.

CHAPTER XIX.

CHAPTER XX.

CHAPTER XXI.

POSTSCRIPT.

APPENDIX A.

APPENDIX B.

APPENDIX C.

ERRATA.

Page 34, *line* 10 }
  ,, 35 ,, 13 } *for* "Tomasio," *read* Tommaso.
  ,, 38 ,,   3 }
  ,, 54, *headline, for* "Boulaq," *read* Boulak.
  ,, 199   ,, }
  ,, 200   ,,   *and line* 22 } *for* "Sonhadj," *read* Souhadj.
  ,, 250, *line* 15, *for* "pyroteconic," *read* pyrotechnic.
  ,, 97, *headline, and line* 13 }
  ,, 99, *line* 24   } *for* "Hekekan," *read* Hekekyan.

** *Oriental words and names, such as* "baksheesh" *and* "Boulak," *admit of great varieties of spelling. The more erudite the writer, the more eccentric to our eyes is his orthography, because he seeks to render the true phonetic value of Arabic, in English, letters.*

PREFACE.

I have made my own journal the basis of the following account of the tour of the Prince and Princess of Wales, although I felt some inconvenience would arise from adopting that course. In the first place, I had to obtain from others the materials for the itinerary of the Royal travellers between London and Alexandria, without which the record would not have been complete. Interpolated between that short chapter, which principally contains names and dates, and the narrative of the voyage to the First Cataract, there is a little sketch of the proceedings of the party with which I started from Paris, and of our life in Egypt previous to the coming of the Prince and Princess.

When I left England, to accompany the Duke of Sutherland and his friends, I had no intention of extending my tour beyond the Nile and the Suez

B

Canal. It had been arranged that we were to await
the arrival of the Prince and Princess at Cairo,
and attend their Royal Highnesses to the First
Cataract in a steamer placed at the Duke's
disposal by the Viceroy of Egypt. Beyond that
there were no definite plans with respect to our
movements.

In the early part of the year the relations between
Turkey and Greece were so threatening, that a
royal visit to Constantinople or Athens seemed to be
impolitic, if not altogether impracticable. If Constantinople could not be approached, of course it
would be impossible for the Prince and Princess to
visit the Crimea. There is no real political incognito in the case of exalted personages; and the Baron
and Baroness of Renfrew cannot make an excursion
from which the Prince and Princess of Wales are
debarred. But the cloud which hung over that
stormy Icarian Sea, where the Eastern question is
riding so uneasily, lifted in spring-time, and the
Royal tour expanded as the sky became clearer.

Whilst the Prince and Princess were engaged
on their expedition, between the First and Second
Cataracts and back, I went on a very hasty pilgrimage to Jerusalem. I have borrowed the account of
their excursion from the note-book of a friend. They

made a more rapid descent from the Second Cataract than was anticipated. Consequently I was compelled to leave Palestine after a brief stay, and to return to Cairo, in conformity with a promise I had made to await there His Royal Highness's arrival, in case he desired, or found it convenient to go to the Crimea. I was fortunate enough to arrive at Port Said on the same day as the Viceroy, and I was invited to accompany him in his inspection of the Suez Canal. On reaching Cairo, I received an intimation from the Prince of Wales that he would visit Sebastopol, and an invitation, couched in the most gracious and considerate terms, to form one of his suite on the occasion. From that period up to the date of the arrival of the Royal party in Paris, on their way home, the narrative is founded on my journal.

It will be readily understood, that he who writes an account of a recent Royal progress in foreign countries, has to encounter difficulties which would not lie in his way if he were travelling under ordinary conditions. It must not be inferred that there was anything to complain of, if I say that the guest of a King cannot very well sit down to criticise the arrangements of the Palace in which he was lodged, as if he were writing of his last hotel—

or that there was anything to condemn, if I remark that he cannot indulge in comments on people he met there, a few days after parting from them, as freely as if he had seen them in the street, or had heard of them by popular report. From a height, one sees more, but he does not make out the details so well as on the plain ; and if his horizon be wide, his steps are limited. But, at the same time, he can observe objects on the summit, which are scarcely visible to those beneath.

If the advantages of visiting strange countries be recognized in the case of private persons, these, whatever they may be, should certainly be largely developed when the stranger is one whose know-ledge of foreign lands, acquaintance with distin-guished men, and intimacy with different Courts, will be turned to account some day when he is the ruler of a vast empire which possesses interests all over the world. Although the direct control of the king be constitutionally reduced to a minimum by our system of ministerial action and responsibility, the influence of the monarch, always considerable, is augmented in proportion to his personal ability and energy; and in many affairs he has, perhaps, a larger and more direct share of management than is generally supposed.

It is of benefit to the country that the true value of political questions and the actual characters of foreign statesmen should be known to the man who is destined to take such an important part as a judicious and strenuous king can always assume, without unconstitutional encroachments, in guiding our administration of foreign affairs. The Prince of Wales has just visited every Court in Europe, except that of Russia, with which he is already acquainted, and those of Italy and Portugal, which are, perhaps, reserved for a future occasion. Spain is courtless. There is not a statesman or politician of note, from Copenhagen to Cairo, with whom he has not conversed, and of whose views on most great questions he is not informed. Their armies, navies, social institutions, religious systems, educational establishments—he has seen something of these wherever he has gone, to his own great profit, and no doubt to the ultimate use of the State.

In the course of our Odyssey there occurred many incidents, there were seen many men, manners, and cities. Some of the men are so near to us—others were beheld under such peculiar circumstances—the manners and cities are so familiar—that it would not be justifiable to transcribe passages relating to

them from a private memorandum-book; but, on
the whole, the narrative of our daily life will be
given without restraint, though I am aware that
there is nothing in many of the scenes, or in the
course of the tour itself, to warrant minute details,
and that it is in the travellers themselves, and in
the circumstances surrounding them, rather than
in their travels, that whatever interest there is in
these pages will be found to centre.

I alone am responsible for any expression of
opinion and indication of feeling which may be found
in the following pages, and in no instance are they
to be attributed to those whose sentiments would
be entitled to the highest consideration. If I have
written with perfect freedom, I have endeavoured
to avoid injury to just susceptibilities. I hope my
readers will pardon any deviations from the subject
indicated in the title, which may arise from the
introduction of personal incidents and recollections.
My recurrence to the aid of friends I feel sure
does not need an apology.

To Professor Owen my thanks are due for a
chapter on the Nile Basin and on the Suez Canal,
from a scientific point of view; to the knowledge
and notes of some I confess my obligations in all
matters relating to ornithology and natural history;

to the accomplished pencils of others I owe the best of the illustrations; and to all my companions, from the highest, I am indebted for unvarying kindness, for a long series of pleasant hours, and for grateful reminiscences of many happy days.

CHAPTER I.

NOVEMBER 17TH, 1868.—The Prince and Princess
of Wales, with their three eldest children, attended
by Lady Carmarthen, General Sir W. Knollys,
Lt.-Col. Keppel, and Dr. Minter, R.N., left Marl-
borough House, on their way to the Continent.
They travelled by the 8.30 P.M. mail train from
Charing Cross Station; and after a rapid passage
across the Channel in the Maid of Kent steamer,
reached the Hôtel Bristol, Paris, a little before
9 o'clock on the morning of the 18th of November.

On 20th November the Prince and Princess
went to Compiègne, on a visit to the Emperor and
Empress. They left Paris at 10 o'clock A.M. in the
Imperial train, and reached Compiègne shortly
after 11 o'clock. The Emperor was waiting at
the station, and conducted his guests in open
carriages through the town to the Palace.

A déjeûner was served soon after their arrival, and
then their Royal Highnesses drove to the Rendezvous
de la Chasse, about four miles off in the forest, for a
stag hunt. Horses were provided for the Prince of
Wales and his equerry. The Emperor did not ride.
About a mile distant the hounds were waiting, and
His Royal Highness having ridden to the spot, they
were turned off.

To ride through the forest was impossible : it was
necessary to go by one of the numerous allées, in
which the forest abounds, in the direction in which
the hounds were running. Shortly after the com-
mencement of the hunt, a curious accident happened
to the Prince of Wales. As he was galloping
along one of the drives, a stag rushed across and
knocked him and his horse completely over. He
got up again at once, and, though slightly bruised
and shaken, remounted and continued on horse-
back till it got too late to pursue any longer.

The stag was not killed till some time after dark.
The curée took place, in the courtyard of the Palace,
after dinner.

On 21st November the Emperor gave the Prince
a day's shooting, the game chiefly pheasants and
rabbits.   There were ten guns out.   The shooting party consisted of the Emperor, the Prince
of Wales, Marshal Bazaine, the Duc d'Albe,
the Comte de Moltke, the Comte Mercy Argen-
teau, the Marquis of Lansdowne, the Comte
Bedinur, General Sir W. Knollys, and Lieut.-Col.
Keppel. His Royal Highness bagged 270 head;
Lord Lansdowne came next, with 260 head, and
the Emperor third, with 239 head.

After the day's shooting was over, the Prince
and Princess returned to Paris, the Emperor and
Empress accompanying them to the station at
Compiègne.

Thursday, November 26th, 1868.—The Prince
and Princess left Paris at 5 P.M., viâ Namur and
Liege, and reached Cologne at 5 A.M. on the
morning of the 27th. They left Cologne in the
evening at 7.15, and reached Hohendorf soon
after 7 on the morning of the 28th. The
passage across the Elbe was effected in a steam
ferry, and a slow train thence brought their Royal

Highnesses to Lübeck in about two and a half hours. At Lübeck they embarked on board the Danish Government steamer Freya, and after a sea passage of about eight and a half hours from Travemunde, reached Korsoer in the course of the night.

Sunday, November 29th.—Soon after 9 A.M. the Crown Prince of Denmark came on board the Freya to welcome the Prince and Princess. At 9.30 they landed, and were loudly cheered by the assembled crowd. They proceeded by special train to Fredensborg, viâ Copenhagen, where they were met by the King and Prince Waldemar. The Queen and Princess Thyra were waiting at the station of Fredensborg, and thence the party drove to the Slot. The Princess of Wales was greatly cheered by the people.

Tuesday, December 1st.—The birthday of the Princess of Wales. At 1.15 P.M. the ladies and gentlemen in waiting and several friends, assembled in the large saloon of the Palace, and offered their felicitations. In the evening there was a large dinner-party, to which Sir C. Wyke, the British Minister, and his attachés were invited. The King proposed in Danish the health of the Princess, saying it was six years since he had had the pleasure

of having her with him on her birthday; and that
when he looked back upon the anxious time of her
severe illness of the previous year, he could not be
sufficiently grateful to Almighty God for being able
to have her now sitting by his side almost completely
recovered.

On December 2nd, and on several subsequent occasions, the Prince of Wales went out shooting. On
these occasions the peasants sent their carriages,
holding three persons, besides the driver, and drawn
generally by a pair of excellent cobs, to take His
Majesty's guests to the shooting-ground. In former
days they were compelled to do so, but now the King
always pays for the carriages he requires.

Tuesday, December 15th.—The Prince of Wales
left Fredensborg, by special train, at 11 A.M. for
Stockholm. The Crown Prince of Denmark accompanied him as far as Helsingborg across the Sound,
which place they reached after a rapid passage of
twenty minutes. The Prince proceeded as far as
Jonköping, where he slept.

Wednesday, December 16th.—The Prince left
Jonköping at 6.45 A.M., and reached Stockholm
at 7.15 P.M. The King of Sweden met the Prince
at the railway station, and conducted him to the
Palace. The Prince remained at Stockholm till

Tuesday, December 22nd, during which time he
was made a Freemason, and was present at a ball
at the Palace, and at one given by Prince Oscar
of Sweden.

On the morning of the 22nd December, the Prince
left Stockholm at 6 o'clock, and was accompanied by
the King to the first station. He reached Helsingborg at 3.30 on the morning of the 23rd, whence
a special steamer and train brought him back to
Fredensborg by 6 A.M., in twenty-four hours after
leaving Stockholm.

Monday, December 28th.—The Danish Court
moved to Copenhagen from Fredensborg, and on 5th
January, 1869, the Prince and Princess were present
at a full-dress state ball at the Christianborg Palace.

January 15th.—The Prince and Princess of Wales,
with the infant Princes, and with Lady Carmarthen,
Hon. Mrs. W. Grey, Sir W. Knollys, Lieut.-Col.
Keppel, Lieut.-Col. Teesdale, Capt. Arthur Ellis, Lord
Carington, the Hon. O. Montagu, and Dr. Minter,
R.N., in attendance, left Copenhagen at 8.30 P.M.
At the railway station the Foreign Ministers and
various officers of Court, in full uniform, were waiting to bid adieu to their Royal Highnesses, who
quitted the hospitable Court and city, where they
had received such genuine kindness and heartfelt

attention, with great regret. To one of them there
was, of course, a special and natural reason for
sorrow. All, without exception, entertained a lively
sense of the warmth of the right royal welcome.
The King and Queen of Denmark, the Crown
Prince, Sir Charles Wyke, Mr. Strachey, and Mr.
Macdonald, accompanied the Prince and Princess
to Korsoer. Countess Reventflow, Admiral Irminger,
Captain Lund, and Captain Bardenfelt, were of the
suite.

It was midnight when the party reached the
port and embarked on board the Freya despatch-
boat, Commander M'Dougall. The King and Queen
of Denmark then took leave of their daughter and
of the Prince, and the steamer, proceeding at once
to sea, lay on her course for Lübeck, which she
reached in ten hours, and where Mr. Moore, the
English Minister for the Hanse Towns, was in attendance. A special train conveyed the Royal party
to Hamburgh at 1.30 P.M. The weather was cold, the
thermometer marking five degrees of Reaumur. The
party, forty-two in all, were put up at the Hôtel
Victoria, where a dinner was given in the evening
to the Duke and Duchess of Glücksburg, the Princess Louise, and Prince Julius of Glücksburg.

On the following day the first token of the long

journey before the Prince and Princess was given
by the departure of the Royal children, who, in
charge of Lady Carmarthen, Sir William Knollys,
and Lieut.-Col. Keppel, left the hotel at 7.30 in
the morning, on their way to England.

The same day, soon after noon, the Royal travellers
left Hamburgh, and arrived at Berlin at 7 o'clock
at night. They were met at the station by the
Crown Prince and Crown Princess of Prussia, Prince
Henry of Hesse Darmstadt, Lord Augustus Loftus,
Mr. Petre, Lord Brabazon, Mr. Frank Lascelles, and
Mr. O'Connor, attached to Her Britannic Majesty's
Legation, and Mrs. Petre, Lady Brabazon, and Mrs.
Frank Lascelles. The weather was bitterly cold,
Reaumur marking eight degrees of frost.

On the following day (the 18th of January being
one of the two days in the year on which it can be
held) a Chapter of the Order of the Black Eagle
was convened, and the Prince of Wales was invested
with the Collar. At 2.30 a procession was formed
at the Old Schloss, Heralds, Pages, Officers of State,
the nineteen Knights Grand Cross entering in the
following order :— General Von Roon (1), Baron
Von Moltke (2), Count Von Redern (3), Count Von
Bismarck (4), General Vencker (5), Count Von Wal-
dersee (6), Count Von Werderer (7), General Von

Bresenniay (8), Prince Adolph Hohenlohe (9), the Chancellor, Field Marshal, Count Von Wrangel (10), Prince Albert of Prussia's Son (11), the Duke of Mecklenburg-Strelitz (12), Prince August of Wurtemberg (13), Prince Frederick Charles of Prussia (14), Prince Alexander of Prussia (15), Prince Adelbert (16), Prince Albert of Prussia (17), the Crown Prince (18), the King (19). All Knights wore their robes and collars; the King alone remained covered. He wore his helmet, and, standing on the throne in the Rittersaal, after a short address, proceeded to invest the Prince, who was introduced by the Crown Prince and Prince Albert, when he had taken the necessary oaths, with the Collar. The whole ceremony was exceedingly imposing, and the brilliant decorations in the hall and the display of old plate very striking.

An early dinner at the Royal Palace permitted the company to proceed afterwards to the Opera House, where they witnessed the ballet of "Sardanapalus."

The weather was so cold that every opportunity was given to indulge in the amusement of skating, and on the 19th and 20th there were very pretty exhibitions at the Thiergarten.

On the night of the 20th January, the Royal travellers left Berlin by the ordinary night express

train, the Crown Prince and Princess, together with
their household, the British Embassy, and many
of the Ministers, accompanying them to the station.

Ten degrees of frost, and a country whitened with
snow, made them sensible of one of the few advantages which the English climate possesses over that
of the dry plateaux of Northern and Central Europe.

It was 8 o'clock at night when the train reached
Vienna. At the station, the Emperor, in full uniform, the Duke of Wurtemberg, the Archduchess
Thérèse, Prince Augustus of Saxe Coburg, the Princess
Clémentine, the Princess Amalie, Prince William of
Schleswig-Holstein-Glücksburg, Prince Hohenlohe,
Lord Bloomfield, the British Ambassador, with the
members of the Embassy, the Danish Minister, and
many others, were in waiting, and received the Royal
travellers, who were driven to the Burg, where the
Empress, attended by the Princess Thurn-Taxis and
the Countess Hunyady, welcomed them, and shortly
afterwards they were left to the enjoyment of repose
in the fine old Castle. The rooms are almost countless, of great size, the floors of exquisite parquet.
In one there is a series of the largest and finest
mosaics in the world, which formerly belonged to
the Grand Duke of Tuscany.

The cold next day increased to nearly fifteen

degrees, and a sharp wind gave an edge to its intensity. Visits, grand dinners, and the theatre, occupied the party during their sojourn at Vienna. Skating, too, had a share in the disposition of the time ; and all the civilities and courtesies in which the Court of Vienna excel were lavished upon the Royal party, and tended to render their stay exceedingly delightful.

The Prince and Princess paid visits to the King and Queen of Hanover in their retirement at Hietzing, near Vienna.

On the 27th January the Prince and Princess left the Burg. The train, which started at 7 o'clock, having passed the Sömmering in all the glories of bright sunshine, arrived at Trieste at 7.30 P.M. The Prince and Princess and suite embarked on board H.M.S. Psyche (Commander Sir F. Blackwood), and went off in her to H.M.S. Ariadne (Captain F. Campbell),* which burnt blue lights and rockets.

Two hours after midnight a terrible fire broke out in the town of Trieste, and all the Royal party were aroused to come up on deck, and look at the raging of the flames, which destroyed a long line of warehouses.

* Captain F. Campbell, A.D.C. to the Queen, was sent out from London to take command of the ship, in consequence of the lamented illness of Captain Colin Campbell, who was obliged to remain at Malta.

The Ariadne got ready for sea, weighed at 9 A.M. on the morning of the 28th January, and proceeded on her way to Alexandria; but her progress was not very rapid. Next day was squally and misty, with a southerly wind right ahead; the speed fell off from eight to six, and then to five knots. On the following day, the speed increased to nine knots, but the wind was still adverse, and the weather cloudy. The next day (Sunday), with a calm sea, and lighter breezes, the Ariadne made good way, passing the Albanian coast, with its ranges of snow-capped mountains, Zante, and Navarino. Mr. Onslow, the chaplain, read service at 11 o'clock. Every hour brought an increase in the temperature; and the usual enjoyments on board ship in fine weather came into play. There were singing and hornpipe dancing, electro-biology and mesmerism, on lawful days, between decks.

At 9 o'clock on the evening of the 2nd of February, the Ariadne arrived off Alexandria, fired a gun, sent up rockets, burnt blue and red lights; but it was too late to try the inner passage to the harbour, which is only safe by daylight.

At 7 o'clock next morning, February 3rd, the Prince and Princess, with their suite, were in readiness to land. Colonel Stanton, H.B.M. Consul-General, came off from the Psyche, accompanied by Sir Samuel Baker, and paid his respects to their Royal Highnesses. The Ariadne steamed into the harbour at 8 o'clock, A.M., all the Egyptian and foreign men-of-war saluting, manning the yards, and dressing ship. The French and Danish Consuls-General, the captain and officers of the French frigate, Mourad Pasha, Abd-el-Kader Bey (attached to the Royal party during their stay), the Governor of Alexandria, &c., repaired on board. At 11.30 o'clock the Prince and Princess left the Ariadne, in the state barge, and repaired to the landing-place, where they were received by Mehemet Tewfik Pasha and Sheeref Pasha, and a great crowd of officials, all in uniform. The Prince of Wales was in his uniform of General, and his suite were also attired in the dress of their rank.

At a quarter past 5 o'clock they arrived at Cairo, at the Kasr El Nil.

So far, the account of the Royal tour has been carried by other hands. Having now seen the Prince and Princess safely into Cairo, I will go back a few days to my own party, which was anxiously awaiting their arrival in the Egyptian

capital, and will give some description of our
doings on the way to it and in it, and of an excursion
on the Suez Canal, which was made in the interval
whilst we were expecting the Prince and Princess
of Wales.

CHAPTER II.

HE Prince and Princess were enjoying the hospitalities of the Northern Courts, whilst the Duke of Sutherland's party, assembled in Paris, were preparing for their visit to Egypt. And Paris is the worst place in the world to start

from after a short stay, for it is the least pleasant
to leave—that is, as long as one has money
in his purse and friends around him. But
at 8.40 on the night of 14th January we departed for Brindisi, over Mont Cenis. We were
six in all, not including the faithful Alister (the
Duke's piper), and the domestics. Our travelling
impediments were reduced to the smallest size and
least weight consistent with comfort. A saloon
carriage—a director or two in attendance—plenty
of room—civil and attentive guards, who kept
the doors against all comers—and great powers of
sleeping, and of contenting ourselves when waking,
made the long route seem short, though nothing
could render it always warm.

Now-a-days men travel by villages and towns very
much as in old times they went past milestones; nay,
they are even less noticed, unless the traveller have
some interest in them. People go and come like
shadows, in the night and the day. The face we
are longing to know more about lightens up as
the train halts at some station, is embraced by
Monsieur as its owner alights, and vanishes for
parts unknown in the interior. And if you take
an interest in the face, what chance is there of
you knowing anything about it? There! As you

are musing or staring, the whistle sounds and
you move off, and in ten minutes are five miles
away, while the face is going off by some poplar-
lined road to Boissy le Sec or Château Belle-
fille. In the old days you might hold a long conversation on the subject ere the horses were put to,
and learn a family history. But these are not the only
differences between now and then, and it would be a
big book which would hold them all. The greatest
interest of the through-route traveller in cities and
stations is now connected with his animal wants.
" Macon at — A.M. Capital buffet !" " Ten minutes
at Culoz." " Try those little game pies, and avoid
the coffee and wine !" And so on.

I do not know whether I would advise any one
unpressed by violent hurry in travelling to take the
Mont Cenis route for choice in winter. It is very
picturesque, very grand, very cold, and not very
comfortable. And if for us it was so, what may it
not be for ordinary passengers, who must not expect directors in attendance, special trains, saloon
carriages, ordered banquets, and accommodation be-
spoken by telegram from the superior authorities ?
In fact, opening a new route across the Alps is
very much like making a new line on the American continent. In the latter case you have to

carry inns, accommodation, and necessaries of life
along with you. In the former, you must slowly
break through the crust of old-established civilization and the hardened forms of torpid life which
have prevailed for centuries—break them down, as it
were, with the buffer of the engine. Old diligences
still linger lovingly here at the stations and at the
termini of the adventurous young lines which climb
mountains, pierce through rocks, cross torrents, and
descend swiftly down Alpine slopes into the far-
reaching plains. The stalactite innkeepers do not
understand it at all. They do not see why people
should be in such haste. They cannot quite meet
the wants of passengers who desire reserved bedrooms
and special accommodation. But they are gradually
warming up to the great fact that people who need
these things must pay for them. St. Michel, where
the party arrived in the afternoon of February
15th, is certainly not a tempting place for a traveller to live in—at least, for more than a day or
two. The situation, indeed, is picturesque. Buried
in one of these Alpine valleys, which eat into
the mountain barriers, as if seeking to find a passage—surrounded by fir-clad steeps and rugged
mountain spurs, growing pile upon pile into the
snow-covered summits—it is shut out for many

hours from the rays of the blessed sun in its
shivering depths. A one-streeted, many-laned,
crooked-housed, rugged-paved place, with a Savoyard
population, regulated by the usual proportion of
booted gendarmerie, a small traffic carried by
enormous barrels on attenuated carts, two gaunt
inns, wine shops, and the various magazines which
supply the wants of a southern French town
introduced into an Alpine village—these, seen
under the influences of bitter wind, clouds of
granite-like snow whirling through street and
passage and window-frame, were not very likely
to lead to warm appreciation of the advantages
of the situation of St. Michel. But, when
the night came, indeed, and the whole party
assembled in a large cavernous room, lit by
cresset lamps, and sat down to a most excellent
dinner, the interior of the Hôtel de la Poste
we found could give better cheer than would
have been anticipated. St. Michel has its master-
pieces of cookery. On the top of Mont Cenis
there is a lake which, even in winter time, yields
store of famous trout. They grow, feeding the
Lord knows how, to the weight of eight or ten
pounds. Pale-skinned, feebly-speckled, large-headed,
unpromising on the outside as St. Michel itself,

they are, beneath the scaly surface, worthy of
the table of kings. And then, too, there is a
very clever dish of Savoyard origin, which, with
the trout, is quite enough for any man's dinner.
But, ascending from the plain to such an altitude,
and meeting so great a change of temperature,
indisposed more than one of the party. "Miserable pain surprised" me. How the night passed,
or the next day, or the day after, I scarcely
remember. I was aware of many kind attentions
from friends; of being animated by feeble hostility
towards beneficent persons who inquired from time
to time how I felt; of gazing, through a haze of
suffering, at beautiful landscapes; of looking through
vales of agony into vast ravines bedecked with rocks
and precipices and tumbling torrents; of passing
through dark tunnels; of making great descents
through covered ways. I have a sort of a cloudy
idea of a reception at Susa, where Count Arrivabene
met the Duke, and a misty notion of a change of
carriages, and of an arrival towards nightfall in Turin,
and of a grand procession, up lighted passages and
corridors in the Hôtel de l'Europe, and of an induc-
tion into a right royal suite of apartments, and of a
mystic visit to the opera. But neuralgia was over it
all. The recollection of the journey is now like that

which one has of a protracted nightmare. Early
next morning—yes,—there *was* a bill. And all I
am glad to say is that it rarely happens to us to
have the privilege of sharing in payment of such
a document ; but then dukes, with gold mines, and
companions, who would have gold mines if willing
could do it, are not to be had at Turin every day.

January 18th.—It was close on 11 o'clock A.M.,
when the train reached Brindisi. We had taken
some twenty-eight hours to make the run from
Turin. What famous places had been passed night
and day by our rattling chariot wheels—Piacenza,
Parma, Modena, Bologna, Rimini ! What fair fat
fields, enriched by many battles ! What world-
renowned sites, dear to antiquary, artist, and
man of letters !—to us now mere notches on the
finger-post of the time-table. Through our route
yesterday it rained heavily, and there were few
workers in the fields, and but small gatherings
at the stations. But still it was known that
an English duke was somewhere about; and the
name he bears is dear to many Italians, who believe
that the friend of Garibaldi must be the friend of
their great idea. At Turin, indeed, when some of our
party went to the opera, it was supposed the Prince
of Wales was present incognito. The audience saw

a fair-haired, blue-eyed Saxon with flaxen moustache
in the box presented by the municipality to the
Duke for the night, and they took it for granted
it was His Royal Highness; and no doubt, in spite
of certain modest retirements on his part, it gave our
friend a pleasurable thrill. "I was taken for the
king," says Müller in the play, "and hang me if I
didn't feel like one!" At Brindisi, however, there
were no doubtful honours awaiting the travellers or
their chief. And, indeed, how could we escape them?
The vessel would not sail till 9 P.M. There was
a great reception. There were municipal bodies, and
sotto prefettos, and magistrates, and civic and port
personages awaiting to welcome "il duca di Sutherland, l'amico di Garibaldi." And they took posses-
sion. We were carried off to the hotel, of which I
shall say nothing, because it is only a makeshift—
the old original tavern, which contented Brindisians
for ages past. There is a new hotel in posse on the
quay—a heap of sand and rubbish and a pile of
timber mark the spot. But till it is built, let
passengers provide store of food, unless they are
content with what they can get—it will be sur-
prising if they are—and let them come prepared for
a sojourn in one of the dirtiest places I ever saw.
The whole nature of the people must be changed,

their habits and customs completely purified and altered, ere the streets of Brindisi can cease to be an offence to civilized human beings. Will "Brindisi farà da se?" It would be so much the better for the agricultural interest near at hand if she would. It will not do to discount the future. Do, dear sotto prefetto, think of this! Passengers will not face present discomforts sustained by the hope of comforts hereafter; and men, and even women, are usually very exacting when they arrive after a long journey by sea or land. Horace—no! not one word of the Iter ad Brundusium this time; nor of Virgil's house, nor of Roman arches and remains, nor of historical reminiscences! After a light repast at the Inn, we set out in two boats to visit the port; and landing at the works on the north-western side of the harbour, beheld a very busy scene—men, boys, and children at work in the quarries of lava-like rock, preparing blocks for transport by the rough rail, to continue the jetty or breakwater which is to complete the harbour. Ragged as Horace's edile, bright-eyed, sallow-skinned, merry enough they seemed, although the taskmasters over the little ones were harsh of voice and prompt of cane. Once, indeed, a young one of the party was so roused by the sight of a

sound whack on a blubbering boy's back that he
was urgent to execute Eton justice on the authority,
and was only deterred by force majeure. As we were
" in charge " of local magnates by sea and land, we
had to do all the works minutely, and to ask many
questions and collect much information. So we
travelled on one of the trucks to the end of the
jetty, and saw the blocks thrown into the sea, which
plashed up eagerly to meet and swallow them, and
admired the sinewy frames and handsome faces of
some of the labourers, who sang in chorus and
cheered themselves in rude rhymes as they toiled.
Then, embarking, we inspected the Citadel or Castle
on the island,—a most interesting memorial of the
old Spanish rule. It contains an internal harbour
for boats and galleys, surrounded by the walls of
the Castle. There were a few soldiers in the place, a
chapel, and some monuments, much desolation and
decay, and a good deal of dirt. On the crumbling
parapet, seawards, there was a newly made gabion-
nade, with traverses ; and a few guns ready to be
mounted, some freshly repaired furnaces, and small
heaps of shot and shell, indicated a purpose of defence
should any Austrian vessel have ventured to attack
the newly created station. For the Brindisians had
" a scare " in 1866. One of the ironclads from the

fleet, after Lissa, might have come down and done just as it pleased, notwithstanding these defences; and no doubt, if the war had lasted, and Trieste had had its way, such a compliment might have been paid. " It 's a splendid harbour !" exclaimed one of our Italian friends. " Some fine day the British fleet might anchor in it."

" That is a long way off," replied an ancient mariner, in a laced cap.—" One frigate was in here some time back, and could scarcely get out again."

" It is easy to approach in all winds," continued the first.

" Except when the wind is strong from the south, or north, or west," said the other.

" Why, a sailing ship can tack in with the wind from any quarter; three-fourths of all the points of the compass, any way."

" If she does not run ashore," quoth the sailor.

" Oh ! you are an Austrian Lloyd's man, and you are prejudiced."

And no doubt he was—a little. For the harbour is better than he made it out, and in the future it is to be all that can be desired, if the plans be carried out—land-locked, with splendid moorings and quays, and deep channels, and good lights. So good luck to the Future. The Italian Government, however, must stretch out a hand to meet it. The funds granted towards the works are nearly exhausted, and the annual vote should be increased.

In the evening the Duke and his friends were entertained at dinner by the Municipality in the Inn, and were introduced to the wines of the country, which were better than might have been expected; and made and heard speeches, ad Brundusii gloriam. The wonderful properties of the Italian tongue were set forth in a remarkable manner by our excellent friend Count Arrivabene, who acted as interpreter; for a few abrupt sentences in English expanded from his lips into rolling orations, which roused burgomasters and subprefects to the highest enthusiasm, and inspired them with great admiration for the eloquence of their guests, the benevolence of their sentiments, and the magnificence of their promises. And so we went out into the street in a blaze of glory, and repaired on board the steamer which lay alongside the jetty. There Captain Vecchini, best of mariners, received us, and, after a warm leavetaking of our warm-hearted and hospitable Brindisians, we prepared for our voyage. There were no other passengers; the ship was all our own. On such an occasion the selfishness of human nature is sure to come out. " How jolly !

We are the only people on board!" Poor Company!
If it were always so, the Brindisi route must soon
close up; but it is seldom indeed such advantages are
to be obtained by a party of friends at the expense
of the Societa Anonima; and I am glad of it, now
I am on shore. There seems every reason for the
line to prosper. Marseilles and Trieste may flourish
too. The world is big enough for all three, and
increase of appetite will grow by what it feeds on.

At 9 o'clock P.M., Il Principe Tomasio steamed
out of Brindisi Harbour for Alexandria. We went
swiftly during the night, and the Captain took
the vessel through the inner passage, between the
islands and Albania, of which we could see the
snow-capped mountains, and the black-looking coast
near at hand, when morning broke. Passing the
Ionian Islands in a short chopping sea, next
morning we saw a few Greek boats scudding
towards shore. "It is different times with them
now the English are gone," quoth Captain Vecchini. "They used to have fine times of it, catching fish, and supplying the tables of those lords at
great prices. Now, they get little or nothing for
what they catch. They regret you, when it is too
late, and find they cannot live upon the glory of
belonging to the Hellenes."

January is scarcely the best time for navigating
the Adriatic.

Our good Captain could not always keep near
land, and, once out at sea, the grégale was upon
us in all its fury, to the great despair of the
Captain, who desired to show how the Prince
Thomas could make a good passage. Next day,
it was still the grégale which blew, and the seas
came swishing overboard, and running downstairs and playing about in the cabin. We
passed Cerigo and Cerigotto, and the Cape of the
Morea scowling through drifting sheets of foam.
The Principe Tomasio can roll under such circumstances, and we were all knocked about, and as
miserable as could be. F. M. suggested a vigorous
policy. Candia was under our lee, but it was fenced
round by jealous corsairs. F. M. advised that we
should run the blockade of the Turk, and take
shelter in any port which lay handy. Whereat
the Captain told terrible tales of Turkish cruisers,
of their reckless firing at everybody, and of his
own captivity once—for the Prince Thomas had
been overhauled and detained, although she was,
he said, far outside the line of blockade. "Who
knows what a Turk will do when he has
got cannon? The only chance we should have

would be that they are all lying snug under cover
somewhere. Otherwise the first warning they
would give us—the brigands!—would be a round
shot; though they seldom hit anything they fire
at." Captain Vecchini had evidently no good opinion
of Turkish, nor, for the matter of that, of Egyptian
sailors either. "How long do you think they would
keep at sea, if they had no European engineers?
How long would they last at all, only they have
money to buy and pay with? They get robbed, of
course they do." And then he tells the famous
anecdote of the Egyptian captain who was ordered
to take his ship to Malta for repairs, and who returned to Alexandria with the statement that there
was no such place as that tight little island. "Malta
mafeesh!" he reported. "There is no such place.
Malta's gone!" And all the time the Captain
was on board a steamer built by Palmer, with
Glasgow-made engines, and Scotch engineer.

But that our party was in a condition of unstable
equilibrium, the voyage might have been enjoyed;
for the table was excellent and well served, every
one willing to please, capital stewards, and all the
means of making life pleasant—if the sea would but
keep quiet! The Captain was held in constant
conversation. "Ask the Captain, please, if he

thinks the wind will go down." " What does
the Captain—ask him—think about Garibaldi?"
That one subject lasted for hours. Then we
diverged to the Papal Government, the affairs
of Ancona, and the bravery of one of our
Brindisian friends, who, as soon as peace was pro-
claimed, challenged an Italian general for a blow
given in active service, and kept a promise he made
to shoot him through the hand which inflicted the
insult. Austria, the Emperor of France, the price
of tobacco and of land, and the future of Italy!
Oftentimes the querists taxed the powers of their
poor interpreter beyond his resources. It is aston-
ishing how little one knows of a language when
he is tried in intricate subjects—especially about
navigation!

One more night—one more day—a night again
—the wind moderating—the party recovering—
that is, the suffering members.

The last day of all became sunny and nearly
calm, though the shoals of flying fish could still
spring from the top of a rolling wave as vantage
for their flight, and the stability of cups and
glasses was not to be confided in.

On the 23rd of January we anchored in Alexandria a little before noon, having maintained our

speed of ten knots an hour on the run. Even now
I shall not be deterred from asserting that Il
Principe Tomasio is a capital boat, though I know
I hurt susceptibilities. All will agree that
Captain Vecchini is a capital sailor. As a worthy
British officer from India wrote in the ship's book :
" I am sure the Captain is a regular brick,
although my ignorance of the lingo he used pre-
vented my having much talk with him." A
Government boat with eight oars came alongside,
and an Egyptian official boarding us, presented the
Duke with an autograph letter of the Viceroy,
bidding him and his party welcome, and full of
pretty compliments. Ali Risa, the officer in
question, speaks English, French, German, Italian,
Arabic, Persian, and his native language, Turkish.
He took charge of the Duke and his friends ; and,
I may fairly say, from that hour, he never lost
sight of us till our departure from Egypt. There
was also the consular dragoman, who must be
as well known as Pompey's Pillar or Cleopatra's
Needle, to lend his voice, his staff of office, the
splendour of his laced attire, and the terror of
his curved scimitar, to the landing, which was
performed with a serenity such as is seldom attendant on the proceeding in Alexandria. How many

thousands of tempers are lost there annually? Who can withstand the temptation to incur the loss offered by porters, donkey boys, beggars, touters, and Egyptian cabmen? Now, they moved in a revolving circle around us, afraid to come within reach, but unable to overcome the force of habit; just like jackals wheeling round a carcase which a lion is guarding. Some Europeans like an excuse for the excitement of assault and battery. It pleases them to indulge in their weakness of "hitting a nigger" with impunity. And nowhere are there such excuses as in this ancient town—ancient, yet very modern.

The population is a very cloaca gentium. It does not flow. It stagnates, and precipitates a villainous deposit. No city in the world contains such a heterogeneous inflow of various races and rascalities. In self-defence, the respectable inhabitants, of whom there are many, are obliged to draw a broad and deep line outside the fortress of their own circle, and good society in Alexandria is difficult of access. The stories one hears of the doings of our Christian friends from some of themselves are nearly inconceivable. No wonder that the Viceroy is anxious to obtain some sort of control over the immigration which finds it worth while to resort

to his dominions, but refuses to obey the laws of
the land, or to be subject to the rule of the
authorities. I am not now prepared to say that it
would be quite safe to sweep away the Consular
Courts absolutely and offhand. Sound guarantees are
needed for the administration of justice between
Egyptians and Europeans. But it is obviously impossible that the present system can go on if Egypt
is to prosper. No country can tolerate, within its
centres of trade and commerce, some dozen and
more of distinct national existences, with separate
and independent jurisdictions, frustrating justice, and
offering strenuous opposition to improvement, refusing to contribute to municipal funds, or in any
way to aid the state by their purses, no matter
how well filled they may be.

A special train was in readiness to take the
party to Cairo; but after so much fatigue, Ali
Risa, who has a profound respect for creature comforts, considered rest and refreshment absolutely
essential, and a banquet was ready, spread by the
adroit hands of M. Joseph at the Hôtel de l'Europe.
We had a drive through the town, visited the
Needle and Pompey's Pillar, and at last, with a
great following of native and European servants in
the Viceroy's employment, started on our journey,

arriving at Kafr e' Zyat in a couple of hours, where another banquet was laid out, and so on to Cairo, which we reached about 10 o'clock P.M.

At the Station carriages and cavasses, and the animated lanterns which precede private vehicles in Cairo—men carrying iron frames on long poles, from which burning tar, coals, and strips of pine throw a bright yellow light on the roadway—were in readiness. In a few minutes the carriages, driving in succession through a gateway into a narrow courtyard, deposited the party at the gate of the Palace. A double line of servants in black received and showed them upstairs. The rooms were a blaze of light. Ali Risa insisted that supper was a matter of the first necessity, and, late as it was, we had to repair to the dinner saloon, where there was another great meal, to which some meritorious persons of the party did ample justice.

The Palace consisted of a large central hall and two corridors, or smaller halls, on the ground floor, the one leading to it from the front entrance, the other leading to the garden at the back, and to the out-offices. Off the first, there were four large rooms, in which the servants lodged. The dinner saloon and other rooms were off the inner passage. From this hall a marble staircase, supported on four

pillars of the same material, ran to the upper
floor, on which, to the right, was a spacious and
handsome drawing-room, on each side of which were
two large bedrooms, one occupied by the Duke of
Sutherland, the other by his son. On the left hand
a similar large room, which was not used for
any state purpose, served to give access to four bedrooms, which were occupied by Colonel Marshall,
Major Alison, Mr. Sumner, and myself. The drawing-room was richly furnished. Satin- and damask-
covered ottomans, sofas, and easy chairs lined the
walls; rich carpeting was spread on the floor; and
the windows were hung with the most massive embroidered silken curtains. But it was curious to see
how recklessly nails were driven into the walls, how
windows were cracked, how doors were left without
paint, and what ruinous legs and backs were united
with frameworks of fine stuff, which had no doubt
cost sums that would have astonished Holland or
Gillow.

CHAPTER III.

January 23rd.—There is a peculiar sound in the air, coming in through the jalousies of the open window. It announces the East at once—an Oriental people, without cares about sewage or rates for the Victoria Main Drain. It is the shrill whistle of the innumerable buzzards—a quavering, not unmusical, note, repeated for the livelong day on all sides, as they flap over house-top and garden. Listen to the cries which come from the street outside the Palace wall, the voices of people always in each other's way, and raised in incessant warning! Veiled women, strings of camels and asses, covered with loads of a certain pulse, on which all the cattle are feasting freely, preparing for the heats of summer —men on donkeys, smoking pipes as they ride— men on foot, with bundles of sugar-cane under their arms; men and women in open carriages and

buggies—all jostling, bumping, and shouting in the
dusty road! The Egyptian, who is more liberal and
civilized than the Turk, is to all appearance far more
Oriental and Mahometan. Reflections cut short by
a tub of water, deliciously cold, also by troubles connected with musquito bites. The sleeping miscreants
being detected as they reposed, bloated and helpless,
on the curtains, inside which they had secreted themselves, met their death. Ali Risa came charged
with messages from the Viceroy, who desired to see
the Duke at 1 o'clock. Then, after undress levées
from room to room, the company assembled for
breakfast in the saloon downstairs. The table was
covered with fruit and flowers, and plate, and
delicate decanters, and fine glass and china, all
marked with the Viceroy's cipher, "I. P." The
attendants — Italians mostly—polyglot, dressed in
black, and wearing the fez or tarboosh. The cooking
excellent; oysters and fish from Alexandria, European
dishes, French and German wines, Eastern pilaffs, and
tiny eggs, and many sweets. After breakfast we went
upstairs to the drawing-room, and pipe-bearers and
coffee-bearers entered in succession, the latter bearing
trays on which stood, in diamond- and ruby-studded
holders of immense value, cups of real coffee; the
others with long-stemmed pipes, having vast amber

mouthpieces, blazing with precious stones, in one
hand, and a metal dish to receive the pipe-bowl in the
other. When an Egyptian takes a pipe, he raises
his hand to his forehead, as a token of thanks. The
bearer inclines the pipe-stem, so that the bowl
shall rest easily on the stand, as the mouthpiece is
held to the lips, and then puts his hand on his
stomach, as a salutation, and retires backwards. The
bearer of the coffee-tray carries on his left shoulder
a velvet cloth or cover, ornamented with golden
bordering, in which are set many precious stones.
These gentlemen were Turks or Arabs, Europeans
not being worthy or capable of such important
charges. When these pipes and coffees had been
puffed and drunk, we descended to the court, where
carriages, driven by coachmen in the gold-laced livery
of the Viceroy, were in readiness, and took a turn
through the city, each vehicle preceded by a running
footman, in richly laced vest and wide white shirt-
sleeves, loose white drawers, cut off a little above the
knee, and leaving the legs bare, who maintained an
eternal cry to the passers-by to get out of the way.
Cairo is undergoing, in its way, a process of Hauss-
mannization. Whole quarters have been pulled down,
and new houses and new streets perplex the traveller
who remembers the ancient places, where he was wont

to walk in fear and trembling through the mazes of the
decayed honeycomb of a city. There is a fine open
space in front of Shepheard's Hotel, and the New
Hotel beyond. Here the Viceroy appears divided
between his desire to form a park and his wish to get
money for building sites; for the sake of the city let
us hope the first may prevail.

Our first visit was made to the river, to inspect
the boats which had been prepared for the expedition up the Nile, those for the Royal party
having been fitted out under the superinten-
dence of Colonel Stanton and Sir Samuel Baker.
The vessel set apart for the Duke and his friends
was the Viceroy's favourite steamer, The Pride
of the Two Seas, and the fastest craft on the
river. She is about the size of a Dover packet,
and draws four and a half feet of water. The
accommodation below, set forth in rosewood and
gold, consisted of a long saloon, at one end
of which was a bath-room, and a small cabin
appropriated to A. S. (by himself) little provident
of the results of its proximity to the boiler; at
the other end two cabins, which were told off to
the Marquis of Stafford and to myself; and then
beyond, a V-shaped divan, on the sofas of which
the Duke and Colonel Marshall made their beds.

By-and-by I will describe how we were lodged,
and give an account of the little flotilla.

Whilst we were at the river-side, we came across
what is called the Arsenal. There were some field-
pieces and gun-carriages to justify the name, but
the main object to attract the attention of the
intelligent foreigner, is a vast collection of
Fowler's steam ploughs, Appold's pumps, agricultural
engines, and various costly apparatus of the kind,
lying in dislocated rusty heaps all over the
enclosure. Cosas d'Egitto! Ordered by Said Pasha, or
some other ruler—found to be in advance of the
age—the cart before the horse—and so left to the
dust and rust. At a rough guess, there was some
£30,000 worth of machinery there. What it cost
Egypt, who can say? I was going to add that
rust, owing to the dryness of the air, was not of
rapid formation in Cairo; but it actually rained a
little this afternoon, and, a few days before our
arrival, a deluge fell on and astonished the city.

At 1 o'clock we drove to the Kasr-el-Nil, or Nile
Castle, and visited the Viceroy. The Palace, which
stands over the water's edge, is full of mirrors, chandeliers, rich carpets, and damask and satin furniture. It
is not large, and, indeed, may almost be described as
being cosy. The view from the windows, out over the

ever-flowing stream, margined by the forest-like masts
of the native boats, and the pyramids of Ghizeh rising
above them towards the west, is animated and interesting. The reception of the Duke's party was of a
most friendly character, and the Khedive was exceedingly gracious to all, for he retains a lively recollection of the efforts made by the Duke of Sutherland to show him attention when he was in England. He expressed the great pleasure he ex-
perienced at the coming to Egypt of the Prince
and Princess of Wales. He particularly desired
that the party should visit the Barrage of the Nile,
the works of which he is about to urge forward,
in the hope of effecting the irrigation of a great
district below Cairo. The visit lasted about half
an hour, and was graced with the pipe and coffee
of honour.

In the evening we went to the Theatre. The
company (French), retained at a great expense by
the Viceroy for the Prince of Wales—remarkably
fat women and lean men—rendered two of the
flimsy little pieces of the Palais Royal, which
seem so attractive to the Cairenes. Not that
the house was very full, although the Viceroy
was present, for, as a rule, the natives are not
yet civilized enough to appreciate French farces.

January 24th.—The early business of the day
over, our courtyard resounded with the cries of
the attendants as they summoned the carriages
to drive to the steamer in which we were to visit
the Barrage of the Nile. The start was not so
easily effected, for the turn into the crowded
street through the gateway is narrow, and our gold-
laced master of the whip took a sharp angle, and
had to draw up his horses in the gateway to
avoid demolition of the hind wheels. He could
not back, for the carriage would have come against
the gate. It was amusing to see the derangement
caused to the attendants by this little catastrophe.
Whilst they were chattering over it, the Europeans,
to the discomposure of Ali Risa, got down and
lifted the carriage wheels, so as to clear the
dangerous portal; and then, heralded by our
running footmen in laced jackets and bare legs
and feet, we cleft our way through the throng
of the busy street very much as a steamer
goes through a shoal of herrings. The shrill cries
of the herald to "Clear the way!—take care!"
act on the mass of people—on the veiled women
and swarming children — like an instinct. They
do not look to see what is coming, but gather
up to the side of the street, and merely glance at

the passing vehicles without curiosity or surprise—without even that half-resentful, half-pleased look which lights up the face of a European who has just escaped being run over.

The streets of Cairo have often been described—that is, painters in words and in colour have made innumerable efforts to convey the impressions produced on the eye by the combinations in architecture, in animal and human life, which are in their entirety quite beyond reproduction, and defy adequate representation on paper or canvas. To add one more to the list of failures in that way, is not a legitimate ambition, though, where so many masters have not succeeded, it would not be discreditable to achieve another fiasco. To my mind there is one great drawback to the pleasure with which the eye would otherwise rest on such an animated scene as every thoroughfare in Cairo affords to the stranger. It is that the population have such a limited allowance of eyes among them. I doubt if there is a good sound pair to be found among every three persons — men, women, and children. Aged and young, it is all the same. The prevalence of ophthalmia, produced, perhaps, humanly speaking, by dust, dirt, and flies, is most destructive to the comeliness of the race; but,

somehow or other, the women of the better class of
lower orders are, as far as one can judge, free from
the worst ravages of this plague, and gaze on the
stranger with a fair share of the organs of vision
above their masked cheeks. The eyes afflicted by
the disease are surrounded by bleared lids, and
are either half-closed or diminished in size, so that
the pupil, dull and whitened with opaque spots, is
like that of a half-boiled fish. The basané tint of
the Egyptian skin is often blurred with the marks of
disease, and the hue would give one the idea that
the ablutions of the race do not extend above the
neck. But the crowds who may be seen washing
in the river, show that they are clean or religious.
The poor children crawl about in the streets and
the doorways like neglected kittens, each the centre
of a swarm of flies, which have their main points of
attraction in the eyelids of the little miserables.
What do they care for that? Has not every one
of them a piece of sugar-cane a couple of feet
long, and perpetually renewed, to chew and suck
at? This is sugar-cane season—men, women, and
children are at it in all directions. People
walk about with bundles of cane six feet long
under their arms, and eat it as it were unconsciously.
A poor wretch is he who has not a couple of yards

au consommation ; and all along the paths people sit in the midst of patches of masticated pulp, and munch the live-long day. In the fields near and inside the city, they are busy cutting it, and loading asses and camels with the mounds of the sweet porous canes. One is at a loss to think what they will all do when sugar-cane time is over. Any way, the practice does not hurt their teeth, which, if we are to judge from what we see, are the whitest, cleanest, and soundest part of their body.

At the present time Cairo is full of pilgrims about to start on their pilgrimage to Mecca, and either it is fancy or fact that the devout people are not fair to look upon. Assuredly they are a long way from godliness, if cleanliness be a mark of approximation to the beauty of Mahometan holiness. Such picturesque, scowling, monoptical old vagabonds look up at the infidels with an unpleasant light in the only visual ray directed against our persons ! They are smoking in doorways, or at the shop fronts, or are slouching in their grandly draped figures (no matter how poor the texture of the robe, it is sure to be well put on)—sombre, grave, if not sad or fierce looking. Sometimes, oh ! horror !—cometh one in a huge pair of horn

spectacles, incongruous with beard and turban.
But be it noted, by the way, that the Egyptian
hereabouts is not grandly bearded like some of
our Indian friends—Sikhs for example; or like
Asiatic Turks and Syrians. At times a blind,

vindictive, but sincere, Mahometan, led by a boy,
approaches, cursing in good set terms all infidels
in general, and your Highness in particular, in
that your domestic has driven him against the wall,

which is not always the place of honour in the
East. I am not quite sure that the ladies, as
being more pious than the men, are not also more
unkindly in look; but it is hard to judge from a
veiled face.

The carriages drove through the gateway of the
Palace, which is also a barrack, and the sentries,
at the sight of the viceregal livery and runners,
seemed in doubt whether to turn out the guard or
not, but gave the guard the benefit of it.

We passed on board the steamer, and were soon
running down the Nile. The wind was exceedingly strong, and by no means warm. But a
terrible fate sits behind the wanderer in distant
lands, and impels him to do all sorts of unpleasant things to himself. The steamer shot by
the Arsenal, where repose in inglorious peace the
implements, which a Viceroy imported without
the workmen, and found too late he could not
work. The lower part of Cairo is not often seen
by strangers now, as the rail has put the old
route by water from Alexandria long time out of
date. But it is worthy of a visit, if it be only for
a view of the tumble-down picturesque old houses,
hanging over the water, ready to fall into it
on the least provocation, and the long lines of

the native boats, with their crews of diverse looks
and sorts, and enormous yards, some more than
a hundred feet long, drawn up by the shore, or
bowling along with the wind, or beating across the
river.   There are also many kiosks and palaces to be
seen, steam pumps for irrigating the land, side by
side with the patriarchal water-wheel and double
bucket.   Much to be admired at is the pertinacity
with which people spend their money in building
walls of masonry, jetties, and quays, by the banks of
the wily and unconquerable old Nile, who bores into
and splits and searches them out in their inner
places, and rifts them up and topples them over.
The ruins abound nevertheless, like most warnings
and awful examples—fruitless of good.   Palace
succeeds palace.   They are only two storeys high,
flat-roofed, with Venetian blinds to the windows,
and very plain outside, being generally washed in
grey, blue, and white; but each has its mirrors,
chandeliers, carpets, and furniture.   Apparently
there is no idea of repairing or doing up one of
these residences.   When a great man's house becomes shabby, he builds him another.

It was most interesting and exciting to watch
the incredible multitudes of wild duck which rose
from the water on the approach of the steamer.

They did not mind the native sail-boats coming
within a hundred yards, but paddled off from
all comers to that distance, and were quite wary
enough to test skill and patience. Among them
were occasionally flocks of geese, which kept by
the shores, some few flights of teal, flocks of pintail
and crested widgeon. One lovely sheldrake on a
bank quite invited a long shot; but we were not out
for sporting; "and let the sportsman note," as old
Izaak Walton says, that this latter end of January
is a trifle too late for Upper Nile shooting. The
duck are now going North, and are congregating
in the waters, between Alexandria and Cairo, where
there is still excellent snipe shooting, as many
as a hundred couple between breakfast and dusk
being possible in some places to a good shot.

In an hour and a half or so we came in sight
of the Grand Barrage, which far exceeded the conception we had formed of it. The project of Linant
Bey, a Frenchman in the Egyptian service, was to
construct two great dams across the two branches
of the Nile, which divides here, and forms a large
island, so as to keep up the level of the waters to
a height which would permit canals cut at the
sides to irrigate the country after the Nile had
sunk below the high-water mark; in other words,

to maintain a constant water-head for the purposes
of fertilizing many thousands of acres. To form an
idea of such an undertaking, we must fancy what it
would be to throw a barrier across the Thames at
Greenwich, in the height of a full tide running
down, with this exception, that the bottom of
the Thames would afford much greater facility for
laying the foundations, for the Nile bed is for many
feet only soft mud. The appearance of the whole
structure is so very light and graceful, that the
spectator is apt to overlook the difficulty and the
greatness of the work itself. The Barrage is archi-
tecturally very beautiful, with a noble front and a
grand general effect, produced by a line of castel-
lated towers which mark the site of each of the
sluice-gates. There are also two lofty crenellated
towers in the centre of the dam, to correspond
with towers over the gateway at each end. The
towers on the right-hand side are constructed with
small sentry-box-like chambers inside; but they
were not used as sentry-boxes, though there was
a guard of soldiers at each end of the dam. As far
as I could count, there are sixty-two arches in the
Barrage. They are made of carved stone, and rise
to a height of some forty or fifty feet above the
river. A considerable number of the sluices were

down, and the Nile was raised six feet above the
level; but in the middle, where the flood-gates were
open, the water was rushing through with immense
rapidity, and in great volume.   They do not
venture to put down all the gates, because the
pressure of such a vast mass of water would, it
is feared, bear down the whole Barrage before
it.   But would that be the case if the intended
canals were ready to carry off the upraised waters?
There is at present only one canal, which irrigates
a portion of country of most fertile character, and
of great importance in consequence of its vicinity
to Cairo, on the right bank.   Why this canal is
insufficient to carry off the water, or whether it be
really so, could not be exactly ascertained, as the
communication between the Egyptian officers in
charge of the works and ourselves was not always
easily established.   But it seems to be the rule to
declare that the Barrage has not done its work—that
it is a complete failure; or, to use the words of Mr.
Murray, that "the works have ended in being a very
useless impediment in the river."   There is a lock
and sluices at the side of the river, on the right
bank, which permit the navigation to be carried on
without any considerable impediment.   Now, in Mr.
Fowler's opinion—which is that most men of com-

mon sense would come to without examining the
question from an engineering point of view and with
special knowledge of the subject—the Barrage must
be regarded as a great work not yet completed, or in
a state of imperfect development, not as a failure
at all.   When the Viceroy's financial position will
permit the execution of the large schemes which he
contemplates for the improvement of the country,
there is reason to think the original design will not
fall short of the full measure of good which it was
calculated it would effect.

The boat was made fast to the side of the
quay of the first of the Dams, where a group of
Egyptian officials connected with the Ponts et
Chaussées awaited us, and behind them a crowd
of syces, with horses, apparently belonging to a
cavalry regiment.   As there was an exceedingly
cold wind, the party preferred to walk along the
Barrage, which is broad, and well protected by a
cement or chunam floor, over which animals and
light traffic can pass easily.   The Egyptian officers
proceeded to show the construction of the sluices,
which are formed of double cones of hollow iron,
in a semicircular form, working on radii of rods
fixed to a central axis at each side of the sluice-
gate.   These double cones increase in size from

the lower part of the curve to the top, and the
lowest, which are the largest, fill with water as they
descend into the bed prepared for them in the
masonry at the bottom of the sluices. The labour
of two men at the crank raised one very slowly
against the great pressure of the water from its
bed; when the gate was lowered, it was easy to
understand the advantage of the curved surface
in pressing obliquely against, instead of directly
opposing, the current. At the other side of
the Dam, near the end of the causeway, a series
of strong earthworks, facing the south and west,
was visible. These works are evidently meant as a
tête-de-pont, and a small amount of labour would
soon make them fit for use in war-time. On the
right of the causeway leading to the Dam, there
is a large native village, in which the soldiers
engaged in guarding the bridge were quartered.
Here were the usual groups of veiled women and
half-naked children, and fellahs, sugar-cane in hand
and mouth. There is probably a toll levied on
the traffic, carriers and passengers, over the Barrage,
for several uneasy-looking people started up at our
approach as if to demand their fees. But the
Viceroy's friends do not pay for anything, and we
passed on, and dawdled about whilst the engineer-

ing details underwent elaborate description and discussion.

Two girls, closely veiled, were walking by the river-side near us. An old Egyptian rushed out of the guard-house, and shouted to them; the young ladies at once turned and shuffled along at a trot into a place of safety. What harm did the ancient man of Egypt suppose we could do to the ladies whom he warned off so peremptorily? We were not all so fair to look upon that he thought their peace of mind was in danger, and they only showed us their eyes through a slit in a black mask with a piece of reed jealously barring the bridge of their dear noses. But so it was, and we were obliged to be content with the aspect of the village from afar, and with observing the manners of certain respectable Moslems, who came one after another to the lock-head, spread their carpets on the stones, and devoutly said their prayers and bowed their heads to the ground, standing and kneeling alternately.

It was a pleasant and peaceful scene; the swallows wheeled around us boldly; the large pied kingfisher flopped into the stream close at hand, and the little ox-eyed dotterel ran along the banks in constant activity. Far away, the tops of the

Pyramids rose above the belt of date palms which
barred the horizon, and the tall lateen sails of
the river-boats glided as if free to steer their
course over field and meadow. But there is not
much time for strangers in the land to take their
ease. Poor victims! if they come so far to see,
why see they must; just as in some country houses
visitors are persecuted by daily programmes founded
on the horrible hypothesis that they must all and
each be always doing something and going somewhere, travellers are presumed to be dissatisfied if
they are ever left in peace. Away back again, over
the Barrage to the right bank of the Nile, where
our steeds await us, and then in a procession, some
preferring the safety offered by a seat on the back
of the placid donkey, others on hard-bitted jun-
keting nags, we canter along a narrow and dusty
road across the Delta to the other great Barrage
which forms the dam across the Damietta branch of
the Nile. It resembles the work over the Rosetta
branch in most respects, but it is in a more
secure condition; perhaps some day, not far distant,
thanks to the new water-works, it will turn out
of vast utility. Just now, however, the object of
the works around it seems to be intended for war
rather than for peace. We were in the midst of

a very considerable military position, in the nature
of an intrenched camp, with a wet ditch and
strong parapets, on which are already mounted
some of the armament. An enemy marching on
Cairo must either mask these works, or take the
chance of leaving a powerful corps in his rear. It
is quite obvious that the city is immensely corrobo-
rated by the existence of the works covering the
heads of the Dams, and by the intrenchments,
within which an army of 20,000 men could be
well covered. Some of our party attempted to
mount the parapet, to get a view of the surrounding country, but they were ordered down by the
sentries. There were hundreds of workmen engaged in deepening and widening the bed of
the canal which is to irrigate the Delta, and
will, it is to be hoped, prove a permanent blessing
to the country—for it is a blessing to have crops
five or six times a year, is it not?—a blessing to
somebody far away, if not to the growers. What
other favours of Heaven may follow who can say?

As in all excursions, as long as we were the Viceroy's guests, there was a lunch to be eaten. We
were conducted to a pleasant little kiosk in a garden
full of trees, where a repast was spread with
the usual profusion—champagne, hock, claret, bur-

gundy, sherry, seltzer water, caviare, curries, pâté
de foie gras, hot and cold dishes of fish, flesh, and
poultry, salads, dessert ad infinitum — coffee and
pipes to follow. The gardener sent in bunches
of flowers, and the table was loaded with mandarin
oranges, apples, and exotic fruits.

A circumstance not in any way connected with
the dessert distinguished our return. The Egyptian
ass is a very useful animal—all asses are useful in
their way; but in no country in the world is
donkey power so largely employed as in the land
of the Nile. No matter what horses, carriages,
and chargers may be in waiting, there is sure to
be a succursale of the humble creature which
bears so much of Egyptian life on its back. So
in this present case, our locomotive powers were
in due course augmented by the accession of a
number of the asses of the land; and on one of
these a learned and valued Professor, who can
clothe a valley of dry bones with flesh, and
open their old skeleton secrets with the keys of
science, sat himself down, and prepared to trot off
gaily, amid the noise of the captains and the
shoutings. But the animal was of a morose disposition—jealous of the paces of the high horse;
bent on teaching the Professor a lesson of its own

on the force of the laws of gravitation. It became evident, from a certain oscillating motion, in
which the Professor's seat on the saddle was the
centre and his head the arc of part of a circle, that
the lesson was likely to come off, along with the
corpus delicti, very soon. Genius is fertile in resources, and so is the donkey boy. The former, in
the person of the Professor, called on the latter, and
the latter called to his fellows, and in a few seconds
our friend appeared with a satrap on each side.
He sat his donkey, as it were on a throne, proudly
and securely, his legs pendulous and sweeping the
ground, his arms cast round the neck of the two
children of Ishmael, one on each side, who preserved his equilibrium as if he were Europa herself.
And thus he gained the end of his land journey,
and alighted amidst the congratulations of his
friends—and who with him and near him are
not?—on his own feet, and at the end of his
journey. After a pleasant ride back to the steamer,
with many salaams to the officials, we proceeded
on our way towards Cairo.

There was a glorious sunset to welcome us,
just as there had been a rainbow of transcendant
brightness and beauty to herald our downward
journey. As its rays brought out the Gizeh Pyra-

mids boldly and sharply, and turned the hue of
the palm trees into deep ebon on our right, they
struck the landscape on the left with many-coloured
fingers; and house, and field, and tree responded to
the touch, and warmed into an outburst of gorgeous
splendour, framed by the waters of the river, on
which were reflected the lower part of the picture,
amid a mass of slender spars and lofty sails.

It was nearly dusk when we reached the city, and
it needed many cries to prevent our chariot making
a Juggernaut-like track through the narrow streets.
In the fields on either side, among the water-courses
and sugar-canes, the watch-fires flickered in the centre
of the family groups encamped there for the night,
with horses, camels, asses, and goats around them.

CHAPTER IV.

January 25th.—To an invalid, who expected to find
an agreeable warm morning to greet him on his
awakening, the weather at 8 A.M. would have been
disappointing. There was neither fog nor frost,
nor raw east wind; but though the air was pure
and light, there was a sharpness in it, which
suggested the use of a warm coat or a brisk walk.
As the road before the Palace, which, by the way,
is also the thoroughfare to the fashionable drive,
is not in first-rate condition, an army of children,
boys and girls, has been turned on to cut down
the hillocks and fill up the hollows. It was painful
to watch the little creatures, toddling about with
baskets of earth on their heads, and bags of the
same held against their stomachs with both hands,

F 2

while task-masters, rod in hand, stood by to
stimulate their energies. Still they seemed merry
enough, and if they did not execute very much
work, they probably gave full value for the few
piastres they received for their labour.

After breakfast, Tewfik Pasha, the eldest son of
the Viceroy, accompanied by Mourad Pasha, came to
the Palace to return the Duke of Sutherland's visit,
and the rest of the party were presented to him.
He is seventeen years of age, of middle stature,
slight, good-looking, with an agreeable smile and
fine dark eyes. He was dressed plainly in the
Turkish-cut frock-coat, with the eternal fez or
tarboosh on his head, and a star on his breast.
Pipes were brought in, but His Highness only
held the amber to his lips, and did not smoke.
The conversation was short, and the incident not
very remarkable; but an interest attaches to the
young gentleman, as he is heir-apparent to the
Viceregal throne under the new dispensation, which
overturns the ancient law, and fixes the succession
in the elder line, excluding the Viceroy's brother,
Mustafa Fazil Pasha, and creating, it is said, much
uneasiness in the minds of the Faithful. That the
change must be salutary in its general effect on the
Viceroyalty cannot be doubted; for of all the mis-

fortunes, in regard to its rulers, to which a country like Egypt can be subject, none, perhaps, are more formidable than intrigues and disturbances connected with a disputed succession. It is feared, however, by those who see the advantages of the change, that in the event of the Viceroy's death, a little pressure, and a great deal of other influence, may procure a new firman from Constantinople.

According to arrangement, the party started for the Suez Canal in the afternoon. There was first a small difficulty to be got over. They were the Viceroy's guests, but M. de Lesseps is King of the Canal, and he had invited Mr. Fowler and Professor Owen to join in the excursion. Although His Highness has a couple of summer residences along the route, he could not give the party the same facilities for seeing the Canal. If they did not accept the hospitality of M. de Lesseps, they would have had to camp out, sending tents and horses and food to various stations; not to say a word of the harassing of governors and deputy-governors, and the trouble about boats and steamers all along the line. The Viceroy gave orders that a special train was to be at the Duke's disposal, and thus the two parties were comfortably amalgamated.

The scene at the station was very strange to a
new-come Europe man. A train was about starting,
and the open cars were thronged by a very vociferous
— nay, screaming — swarm of Egyptians, Turks,
Syrians, and Arabs, who struggled for places with
the utmost apparent ferocity, but submitted at once
to the law of the stronger. This was frequently
administered by the servants of the railway, through
the simple agency of a thick stick. Wonderful
was the strange noise which rang out of the
skulls of most respectable-looking persons on the
application of this cogent bye-law ; and admirable
the submissiveness and peace produced by the second
or third decision of the court ! There was as much
shouting on the platform as in the carriages. Certain of the latter were shut in and latticed closely,
being reserved for women of rank, simple enough
in their tastes and food, judging by the supplies of
dates, oranges, and water, handed in through the
windows by their sable attendants. The women
sat crouched in groups by themselves, and did not
always leave the men the squabble-making and controversy. Sundry stolid religieux, bound for Mecca,
with all their goods in a bundle the size of a hat-
box, and with a water-bottle and some dried beans
as their sole viaticum, regarded the confusion as a

part of the sufferings to which the pilgrimage is
subject. It is surely a thorn in the flesh of the
staid stay-at-home Moslem, that they should be
obliged by their faith to undertake such a distasteful
journey as soon as they can afford it, after paying
all just debts, and providing for their wives and
families.

At the station, M. de Lesseps, who was accompanied by Count Waldstein, M. Voisin, M.
Le Clercq, &c., met the party, and the special train
got off at 2.45 P.M. for Ismailia. The route of
the new line, which bisects a triangle of land
between the Nile and the old rail, affords a daytime
passenger an excellent opportunity of seeing the
best part of a fertile and well-watered district.
M. de Lesseps was of course irresistible. He
proves as conquering when he deals with mind as
he has done in his conflict with matter; and as the
train rattled unevenly towards Ismailia, he made
the Desert smile with his fanciful, and perhaps well-
founded, dissertations on the land of Goshen, the
route of the ancient Israelites, the wandering of
the Tribes, and his treatment of similar topics which
the locality was likely to suggest.

It is impossible to do justice to Ismailia now.
Wait till we come to it somewhat later, when the

Paris of the desert was dressed out to welcome the
Viceroy and the Prince and Princess. And then
it will not be easy to give the least idea of the
strange effect of this toy city in the wilderness.
The French made, in a few months, a little Paris at
Kamiesh, in the Crimea. They established right-
angled streets and police; whereas at Balaclava
and Kadikoi, as at Donnybrook, higgledy-piggledy,
tempered by the Provost Marshal, was established.
Kamiesh is a Tadmor, fourteen years old, in
ruins. What may Ismailia become? There is no
germ in it of long life, perhaps. But it is a
pretty butterfly. And may it live a thousand
years! It was evening—6 o'clock—when the train
reached the station. There were horses and carriages, with broad wheel-tires, to travel over the
sands, and a whole host of French gentlemen
connected with the Canal, who came to welcome
M. de Lesseps and his guests. In a few
minutes we were all settling down in various
chalets, to prepare for dinner. In front of my
window there was a boulevart parallel to a sandy
beach, against which waves were breaking with a
gentle rustle, and a lighthouse near at hand cast
its rays, paled by the moon, over the water. "What
is that? Is it a sea, or is it a fresh-water lake?"

"Neither, Monsieur. It is Lake Timsah, which they tell me is Arabic for a crocodile. I remember when all you see was quite dry, but it is now thirty feet, aye! and forty deep, in places. It is filled from the Mediterranean, and the water is salter than that of the sea itself, but it is full of fish. It was made by M. de Lesseps."

At dinner there were some forty persons present, among them two officers of a French frigate, which has been carefully exploring the Red Sea, and has found out an excellent channel free from reefs, rocks, or shoals, from Suez to Aden.

Next morning, early—too early for most of us— we were awakened, and descended to a light meal of coffee and bread, and as 7 o'clock struck, we were on our way to La Mathilde, a little steamer, which was to take the party to Port Said on the Mediterranean. It was a Canal day indeed! Never were men so plied with questions. There were M. de Lesseps, M. Voisin (who is a Bey, by the bye), and M. Guichard, and M. de la Roche, and M. Le Clercq, and sundry others, to each of whom was attached a sedulous Britisher, bent on informing his mind and finding out some weak point in the Canal, and full of doubts and suspicions. The perseverance of these gentlemen

was not, however, too much for the temper and
tact of the French officials. Mr. Fowler began
to admit that the engineers knew their business,
and that they had accomplished a great deal—nay,
that the Canal was "a very considerable work."
In the evening—an hour before sunset—spires
and masts were visible above the level banks,
and beyond them the sea.

The masts and the spires marked the site of
Port Said.

Two large full-rigged ships in the inner basin
were dressed out in flags in honour of the
strangers. The vessels belonged to Russia and
Great Britain, and were laden with coal from England, which can be got at Port Said for 44 francs
a ton. This "caused to reflect" one of our party,
at all events, whose bill for three days' chauffage
in his room, at a very good, but rather exalted,
hotel in Paris, was equal to what he would have
paid for one and a half ton of coal here! There
were, in addition to the ships, one large bark,
twelve brigs and schooners, and a fleet of small
craft, feluccas, &c., giving a great show of activity
and life to the port. As the Mathilde entered
the inner basin and glided onwards towards the
outward harbour, which lies between the two great

arms of masonry extending into the sea, there was
full opportunity to contemplate and admire the
extraordinary progress of this singular enterprise.

Having run down past the Western Pier, the
steamer turned and made for the shore end of
the Eastern Pier. Here we landed and inspected
the vast — for they are vast — preparations for
making the blocks of artificial stone for the piers.
M. de Lesseps pointed out to Professor Owen a
shell imbedded in one of the blocks, and exclaimed, "There, Professor! There's a curious
fossil! Can you make out the epoch of the formation?"

"Oh, yes!" replied the Professor. "It's what
may be called a very recent formation indeed. I
know it, though I have not seen it before. It's la
formation Lessepsienne."

Embarking in boats, we were landed at the
other side of the Port. Here there was a Lighthouse to be visited, which casts its rays out to
sea, to guide the voyager to this port, as yet
unmarked in many charts, yet destined, perhaps,
to a great future in the commerce of the two
worlds. It was well worth while to climb the
tortuous staircase and look down from the lantern
gallery on the newly created town, which has

sprung up as if some great conqueror had ordered
an Alexandria to be founded anew. To the north
lay the long arms of the port, thrown out lovingly
to catch the coy commercial beauty which seemed
so little likely to spring from the foam. The sad
sea-shore extended east and west, marking its limits
on the belt of sand which separates the Mediterranean
from marshy salt lagoons, and the placid waters of
Lake Menzaleh, by a line of breaking foam. Below,
the town of Port Said, spacious and sandy streeted,
enclosing the basins in which float the ships which
have found out a new emporium, and the canal, like
a broad street, thinning away between its banks,
southward, into a thread. The wind blew sharply
from surly Europe, and we descended with alacrity
to find shelter in the comfortable residence of the
Chief of the Section, where we enjoyed all that
hungry and weary men could expect in far better
known and more luxurious cities. After dinner the
moonlight tempted us to visit the City. Miraculous
are the efforts that Port Said has made to assert
itself as a civilized place. Dominoes, billiards, beer,
cigars, and music can be had by those who want
them! It was observable, however, that certain
men with bludgeons were not dispensed with as
guardians of the night; and the Oriental character

of the streets was sustained by the dogs, which
gambolled and growled in the moonlight, unvexed of
infidels. In a little café which we entered, there were
two groups of men, drinking beer, playing dominoes,
and smoking cigarettes, of such quaint attire and
ruffianly aspect that they would have made a reputation for a London ballet-master. With a moonlight strong as day blazing in on us, we retired to
sleep, deeply impressed by the greatness of the work
we had seen, and not at all sorry that the duty of
seeing so much of it had been successfully terminated.

January 27th.—The wind was blowing strongly
from the west over a cold grey sea, scarcely lighted
yet by the faint light from the clouds in the far
east when we were roused from sleep. "M'sieu de
Lesseps!"—(for M. de Lesseps is partout here)—
"il faut éveiller ces Messieurs."   And, Messieurs
rose accordingly, each in his own frame of mind,
as the steps and taps and voices of his awakener
aroused him to a sense of his situation and duties.
My window looked out on the side of the "city,"
next Lake Menzaleh, facing the south-west. There
lay a great expanse of dark slime, which might be
taken for a lake dotted with sand-banks, the seeming
banks being really patches of water, on which the
dawn cast a strange reflection. This stretched away

to the horizon, and as the light grew stronger
the early cranes and flamingoes became visible
stalking about in search of unlucky crustaceans
out too late at night or up too soon in the morning.
Near at hand and bordering the lake a belt of
sand extended between the houses of the town,
and this was spotted by groups of dogs, or by
isolated figures of pious Moslems waiting for the
first ray of sun to begin their prayers. Draped
figures passed, hurrying from the Arab quarter towards the workshops, wrapped up in their bournous
to keep them from the biting wind; for the air
nipped keenly. The sun did not shine out, but the
bell of the principal workshop announced the hour at
which all in Port Said who had work to do—and
who had not?—must get up. Straggling down
at intervals, each member of the party came to
his breakfast of café au lait, bread and diminutive
eggs; and those who came last found that their
predecessors had acted on the principle of "first come
first served," and had remembered the great precept
of "Aide toi et Dieu t'aidera."

Before 7 o'clock some enthusiasts were already
improving their minds and their French by a
walk on the western jetty. Our charming temporary
residence faced the sea, and gave us a view of the

roller-like waves beating against the long line of the
jetty, and of sheets of foam flying over it. In the
garden at the rear, the marvellous effects of fresh
water on the Desert soil were visible in the
groups of bananas, of rose lauriers, and flowering
plants neatly disposed in bordered plots, and fed by
small rigoles from the central reservoir of water,
furnished by pipes all the way from Ismailia. The
trees and plants were moderately healthy looking—
some, indeed, fine and vigorous—but the leaves of
the banana are easily torn by high wind, and have
nothing of the trim conservatory air about them.
From the tall chimneys of the factories volumes of
smoke mingled with the dust, and the clang of
machinery and hammers rose above the moan of the
waves on the beach. The shops were open as we
marched through the fine soft sand which rises to the
instep towards the ateliers and chantiers. There is
the " Grand Café de France." Menazet, Coiffeur,
who sells " postiches pour dames," is shaving an
early and an ugly customer of unknown nationality. Billiards and dominoes are yet asleep, but
various persons, who might have just left off playing at them, are not; and what with the dogs
romping in the streets, and groups of Arabs crouched
about the sheds and in the front of stalls of provi-

sions, Port Said has a busy air; though seawards there is only to be seen a solitary steamer plongeur depositing its load of sand far outside the jetties.

As it was desirable to get in good time to Ismailia, we were obliged to forego visiting the Hospital, the Church, the Cemetery, and the Arab village. The latter lies to the west of Port Said, and contains about 3,000 souls, to which large accessions are being steadily made.

It was 8 o'clock when we got on board **La Mathilde**, which lay alongside the jetty with her steam up; and having bade good-bye to our friends, we set out on our way to Suez. It strikes me that the name of Port Said was a mistake. To most Europeans the words give the idea of a mere "port," a place for landing and embarking goods. The name is due to the desire of M. de Lesseps to pay a compliment to the late Viceroy, who was such a patron of the enterprise. It will not be easy to change it now, and persons who do not find Port Said in Guide-Books or time-tables, will be astonished to hear that nearly 100 sail of foreign vessels came into the harbour last year, and that this very day, when we leave, three steamers—one of the Russian Company, one of the Messagéries Impériales, and one of the

Austrian Lloyd's — will arrive to land and receive goods and passengers.

The return voyage to Ismailia along the Canal presented no unusual incidents. For ever the same annular sand-hills bound the banks, dotted by Arabs and fellahs, who find it pleasant walking by the side of the water, and cream-coloured mounds which hide the desert at each side — the same succession of dredging machines and their attendant flats and boats. We had proof of the speed of the lateen-rigged Arab boats in smooth water. Two of them kept ahead of La Mathilde for more than five miles, though the steamer was making thirteen kilometres an hour. The Arab steersmen enjoyed the contest with sombre delight. Each tried to jockey the other and take his wind in the most approved fashion; but when the steamer, panting and puffing, overtook first one and then the other, it was too much for the feelings of the helmsmen; and they turned their backs, in order not to behold the victory of the infidel contrivance over the plain sailing and homely agency of the wind. And so to Lake Timsah and Ismailia once more.

Thursday, January 28th.—Not quite so early a start as usual this morning. There was an excellent

breakfast to fortify us against the day's fatigue, and
at 8 o'clock we were on our way to the La Mathilde,
which was lying at the little jetty of Ismailia.
What is that we see on board? A tartan plaid
cloak, and a smart little riding-habit! Look again,
there is still another riding-hat, and another cloak.
And listen! There is the ringing of silvery laughter.
M. de Lesseps has filled the Desert, not with flowers
and with pleasant watercourses only.

The Mathilde dived her bow at once into the
bright briny waters of Lake Timsah. It is not
possible by words or painting to give an accu-
rate impression of the newly created sea which
has found out its ancient bed. It is in parts
three-and-a-half miles broad; but longitudinally
the expanse is broken by numerous islands and
sandbanks. Grebes plunged deep at our approach,
flocks of wild duck fluttered along the surface and
squattered down at a safe distance; the boats of
Greek fishermen were busy near the shore, and the
smoke of the bateaux plongeurs streaked the sky.
The surrounding Desert, hillocks of sand, dotted
with tamarisks, spread to the horizon. As we drew
farther away, Ismailia stood well out against the
background, and formed a fine object in the strange
landscape. The tall factory chimney, the white

verandahed houses, the front of the street facing
the lake, gave the idea of a fashionable sea-side
watering place.

The Fresh - Water Canal runs close by. At
times we see the sails of the boats which are using
it as a highway to Cairo rising above the desert
level. We now enter the cuttings from the Lake.
The Canal here is dredged to six metres deep,
and is twenty-two metres broad at the bottom.
Huge banks of very light sand rise high on either
side. There is, no doubt, some danger in this;
but the Desert is covered with tufts of low
brushwood, and it is hoped that some growth
of arenarian grasses, such as there is on the Dunes,
may be established, to check the flying clouds. As
yet we are assured no positive injury has been ex-
perienced from them. We pass a once dilapidated
tomb—now renovated by the pious care of French
engineers—which marks the resting-place of Sheik
Ennedek, of whom I regret to own I can say nothing
except that he was a holy man, and that his memory
is much venerated. Even now it is not a very imposing structure, as it might be easily mistaken for a
whitewashed molehill or a primitive oven; and as
it stands alone in the Desert, a little way above
Toussoum, it is not likely Sheik Ennedek will

ever have occasion to anathematize the disturber
of his ancient bones.   In half an hour the party
came to the end of the Canal southwards from
Lake Timsah.   The cutting here is very deep—
some seventy feet apparently; and the water floated
a large dredging machine, which was biting busily
away into the bank before it, and casting the
earth and sand into the barges, which were to
carry it away and deposit it in Lake Timsah.
There were many of these barges on their way to
the lake, as we came down the Canal.   The sight
of this machine, working its hardest, was very interesting.   The way it is brought to bear on the
bed of the Canal is not novel to engineers, but to
ordinary mortals it seemed most ingenious.   The
earth and sand at the end of a section are first cut
down and carted away by men, camels, asses, and
mules, till a flat surface, the breadth of the canal, is
left, a few inches above the water.   The dredge is
brought up to this, her anchors are carried inland
and firmly fixed, the machinery is set to work, and
speedily the edges of the buckets, tooth-like, bite in
and fill their stomachs with the earth.   As we landed
from La Mathilde, a proof of the immense energy
of fishes in seeking new pasture, and of their enterprise in exploration, was afforded to us.   A couple

of Greek or Italian sailors were casting a net close
to the dredge, within a few feet of the fast-yielding
bank. At every throw the net came up with a fair
haul of fish. They varied from ½lb. to 3lb. each,
and consisted of five distinct species—one, a large-
eyed, very deep fish, with broad scales, like our
sea carp; another like a sea bream; and two which
looked like varieties of grey mullet. Professor Owen
did not see them, I think, and I am not able to
assign their true character. These fish had groped
their way from Lake Timsah, and as that lake
was filled from the Mediterranean, very soon there
will be between the fishes of that sea and of the
Red Sea a meeting, after many roving years, of
those that had been long estranged, which may
prove most distressing to future geologists. Who
knows what M. de Lesseps may have to answer
for on that head? A visit to the fish markets
at Alexandria and Suez enables one to appreciate
the vast difference between the denizens of the seas
of the middle earth and those which swarm in
tropical waters around their coral reefs. It is
evident the fish of the Canal will make acquaintance with strange bed-fellows on the spawn-
ing grounds. Maybe the shark, now a visitor to
the Nile, and a visitor, *parcus et infrequens*, to

the waters of Alexandria, will take a turn up and down the Maritime Canal ere long.

At Serapeum the preparations for turning the bed of the Bitter Lakes into a series of inland seas were going on with activity. The principal object of the engineers is to construct a dam-head to arrest the flow of the waters from the Mediterranean through Lake Timsah, and to form an enormous reservoir from which the overflow will be discharged into the Lakes. Careful investigations have led to the conclusion that it will need about five months to fill the enormous area of the Bitter Lakes, so as not to damage the works, or impede the progress of the labourers in the other parts of the Canal. It is a vast enterprise to let the waters of two oceans into a basin upwards of 100,000 acres in extent.

The party mounted horses and made for Chalouf, to which we came after a pleasant canter over the Desert. The station consists of a few houses of wood, and workshops, erected on a small plateau of sand. Here there have been some very curious remains dug up—sharks' teeth (one of which Professor Owen carried off with glee), wood-work apparently belonging to an ancient sluice in the Canal of Pharaoh Necos, some hieroglyphicized tablets, and a part of a monolithic image. It may be noted that

a traveller will find the sign-board at any rate of a
"Hôtel du Canal Maritime" there.   It was 1.30
P.M. when we halted, and after lunch we mounted
our horses once more, and rode to the station of the
Suez railway, where we bade farewell to the fair
ladies, whom we most likely were never to see again,
and watched them flying at full speed over the
Desert back to Ismailia, till they were hid by the
intervening sand-hills.   The party crossed the old
canal of Pharaoh Necos (Darius' Canal), which has
been filled with fresh water, and a special carriage
and engine took us on towards Suez.

Sails and boats were visible on our left, where the
Fresh-Water Canal and the Maritime Canal run
almost parallel to the railroad.   To complete the
civilized air of the place, once sacred to solitude,
sand, simooms, and Bedouins, telegraph posts and
wires flank our course.   Once more, after a run of
half an hour, we left the railroad, and, mounting
a fresh set of horses, proceeded along the line of
the Canal works to Suez.   They presented a very
striking picture.   The work here is very much
like that in the northern sections, when the Canal
was first begun.   Salt blocks, and earth, and sand,
and stone are being cut away, by the incessant
exertion of upwards of 7,000 men.   The course of

the Canal is marked out in sections, separated by
dams of various thicknesses and heights. As we
rode along the bank, formed of the earth excavated
by these hybrid multitudes, we beheld such a scene
of activity as Egypt never saw since the days of
the Pyramids. A Londoner may form some idea of
it by a peep into a great cutting of the Metropolitan Railway—if he fancies it ten times as broad
and five times as deep, and fills it in his mind's eye
with camels, asses, and half-naked Gentiles from all
the swarming multitudes of the East. At intervals,
on the banks, are fixed steam-engines, which drag
up laden carts on one line of rail to discharge their
contents over the rapidly increasing embankment
at each side, whilst the empty carts are let down on
another line of rails by a chain, so that the two lines
are worked simultaneously. The soil is of a mixed
character. Sometimes there is a section of clay, like
that of the Lower Nile bed—sometimes calcareous
limestone—sometimes sand; the amount of infil-
tration between the beds necessitates the use of
engines to pump out the intensely salt water. The
native workmen often sleep in the recesses, or in holes
cut in the side, of the banks they have made,
covered with loose planks. At every hundred paces
or so there is a rude cabin made of nailed deal

boards, in which the European, whatever he may be
—Frenchman, Italian, or Greek—has his domicile.
For seven or eight miles we rode along the
bank of this curious highway, crossing culverts,
riding under water ducts, where the steam-engines
were pumping out water or letting down trucks, and
continually intercepting lines of asses and camels
passing up and down the incline between the top of
the bank and the bottom of the Canal. At last, far
away, the high mountains over Suez came in sight,
and presently we beheld the masts of ships in the
road, and the houses of Suez itself. A few minutes
more, and we see at the end of the vast trench the
great arm of an elevator, which must be afloat.
Again a few minutes, and there lies a filled canal
before us. We dismount and leave our horses to
the syces. There is a steamer waiting at the dam-
head. We embark. A few kilometres more, and
there comes another dam in view. We land here,
and walk along the bank of the Canal, not yet filled,
but deeply cut and scooped out, and alive with
labourers. From the top of the bank a wide
expanse of sand, now and then submerged by
the sea, stretches away to Suez on our right. On
the left, across the Canal, a sad fawn-coloured
desert spreads over to the hills which rise above

the undulating lowlands of Arabia. It was almost
with a sense of awe we looked at the Red Sea far
away, waiting so tranquilly to be let in to its old
domains. Our walk is terminated by another dam,
at the far side of which there was a canal filled
with water, on which several elevators were busily
engaged. Here two steam-launches awaited us. We
embark once more. This time we are at the end of
our journey.

"Messieurs! nous flottons maintenant sur les
eaux de la Mer Rouge!" The sun had set in a blood-
red arch over "the Plain of the Wandering" ere we
embarked, and our course down the Canal was only
lighted by the lanterns in the vessels. But the lights
of Suez could now and then be seen astern of
us, on our starboard side. The steamers were
fast, and in less than an hour we had turned
the end of the long jetty which runs into the sea
and marks the course of the canal, and passing
the Arab dows and native boats which lay along
the course of the newly-formed pier on the western
side of the entrance, landed at the Hotel Pier.
What a change in Suez since I saw it in 1858!
When the canal works began, there were only 3,000
people in the town. There are now 20,000, and
the greater part of the increase has taken place in

the last year and a half. The last time I was here
one Egyptian sloop of war, a sailing vessel, a few
Arab dows, and one Peninsular and Oriental steamer,
were in port. There were visible, by the light of
the setting sun this evening, five large steamers
belonging to the Messagéries Impériales, two French
frigates, a French corvette, a French gunboat, one
Egyptian passenger-ship for pilgrims to Jeddah,
five Egyptian men-of-war, and H.M.'s transport
Jumna, with troops from Bombay. Ali Bey was
waiting to receive us, for we were once more the
guests of the Viceroy. The dinner was worthy of
one of the best hotels of Europe, the wines excellent, and when the banquet was over we were informed that there was—in Suez, mind—an excellent
café chantant, where French artistes were delighting
a polyglot fez-capped public with the latest Parisian
songs à la Thérèse.

January 29th.—The early part of the day was
devoted to an examination of the Suez Canal Company. Indian passengers of a few years ago will
remember the great spread of sands just awash at
low tide, between the hotel pier and the roadstead
where the Peninsular and Oriental steamers were
wont to anchor. Well, there is now cast over this
a line of railway, not yet open, but nearly ready

for traffic, which will take goods and passengers to and from the docks in course of construction. There is also a causeway extending almost parallel with the railroad to the establishment where the Suez-Canal Company has formed a basin for its floating matériel, with extensive offices. Here, among other curious things, may be seen heaps of wooden fragments of ships, about which M. de Lesseps has his own theory. As they have been carried up by the dredges, from places not far apart, it is just possible they may be the wrecks of the caravels which were sunk in a famous sea-fight off Suez, some 400 years ago, when the Portuguese, rounding the Cape, found their way up here, and were encountered by the Venetian galleys and the fleet of their Turkish allies.

The Bassin de l'Arsenal is well worth a visit. A dry dock, upwards of 400 feet long, has been made by order of the Egyptian Government. This dock is but a part of Port Ibrahim, but the works on the basin are apparently suspended. It was suggested by the Messagéries Impériales; and the Viceroy, who desired to have the means of repairing the vessels he keeps in the Red Sea, gave them permission to make a contract for the execution. They employed M. Dussaud, whose name is well

known in connection with the great undertakings
at Cherbourg, at Marseilles, and at Smyrna. The
manner in which the dock has been executed does
credit to the firm. There was now a large Egyptian
vessel in it, and Captain Pickard, of the Jumna,
told us he had taken her in and found the dock
of great use. Whilst the party were going over
the works, they were joined by Djemali Pasha,
the Egyptian admiral, a smart little man in new
uniform, the effect of which was somewhat impaired
by his drawers falling down over his shoes. But
for his fez he might have passed muster for a
European flag-flier. With him were some Arab
officers and sailors, one of whom eyed me with
great suspicion as I was entering little notes in
my drawing-book. At last his feelings were too
strong for him; he stole behind the Admiral,
pulled his coat-tail, and directed his attention to
my proceedings. The Admiral looked, shrugged
his shoulders, and went on with an expression of
face which seemed to say, "I can't help it if they
blow up the whole port!"

If the Suez Canal Company were the national
representatives of France, the Government of the
Viceroy might find ground for apprehension. The
extremity of the extended railway, the mercantile

terminus, the embouchures of the Canal, will be
in the hands of the Company. The entrances to
Port Ibrahim will be free towards the sea, but
towards the north-east they will be in connection
with the naval establishment, as it may be called,
of the Suez Canal Company. It is perfectly sure,
however, that not only cannot the Suez Canal
Company go to war with any one, but that war
would be one of the most terrible disasters that
could befall the shareholders.

Having inspected the basins and docks, the party
embarked in a little steamer and ran out to the
Jumna, which was filled with drafts of the 77th,
88th, 38th Regiments, &c., and some artillery
from India. The ship was as clean as a transport
can be with 700 men on board; but the pale faces
of the men, and the wan white children, told their
tale of barrack life in India. There was scarcely
a ruddy cheek, and many a very white one, among
the whole of the poor fellows. As we were on the
main deck, a little girl ran out of a group of play-
fellows to a hospital orderly, and exclaimed in
triumph, "Oh! I've seen the dead man! I've seen
the dead man!" The Red Sea exacts heavy tolls
from the homeward bound.

There was just time on our return to shore to

take another run through the bazaars, which still
present a good picture of Oriental life. The old
back streets are wonderfully tumble-down and picturesque, but the main thoroughfares are Judaized,
and Chinese pictures and Paris photographs are to
be had, which it would be much better not to
have.

At half-past 2 the party left Suez by special
train, and arrived in their quarters at the Palace
on the Schoubra Road, Cairo, soon after 8 o'clock.

Everything just as they left it; rooms, servants,
lights, banquets. Ali Risa went off to the Viceroy,
to render an account of the trip. The excursion had
afforded amusement and instruction to every one of
the party, varying, indeed, in kind. Mr. Fowler
was full of engineering facts and interesting details.
Professor Owen had added, if that were possible,
to the stores of his scientific knowledge. He had
beheld with rapture the impress of a bare foot
upon the desert sand, which he said filled him
with particular emotion, as it gave him an idea
how the marks read now with such interest were
made millions of years ago in primeval Sandstone.
Each entertained a different shade of belief, respecting the work itself; and if the sanguine
regarded the Canal as a fait accompli for the 15th

of October, others postponed the date, and believed it would take much more time and money
ere the triumph was achieved. But all were impressed by the magnitude of the undertaking, and
admitted that it had attained a development for
which they were not prepared. In acknowledging
the candour and courtesy of their late companions,
there was a natural regret that, from various causes,
our countrymen had been led to look on the enterprise with a feeling stronger than coldness, and that
to France, or at least to Frenchmen, would belong
the great renown which must follow from the com-
pletion of the Canal that promises to do so much
for the civilized world.

CHAPTER V.

FOR some days, whilst waiting the arrival of the Prince and Princess of Wales in Cairo, we had nothing to do, except visit places of interest. We knew the Ariadne had left Trieste on the 27th, and that she was contending with the waves of the Adriatic.

The delay afforded opportunity to make purchases, to inspect bazaars and mosques, and to partake of the hospitalities which the Viceroy was bent upon dispensing.

Dining with Count Waldstein, one night, I had the pleasure of making the acquaintance of Hekekan Bey, an Armenian gentleman resident in Cairo, whose name is mentioned in almost every book or letter written about that city. Formerly in the service of the Viceroy, he has retired in his old age, yet green and vigorous, to pursue his researches after the mystic meaning of the old Egyptian

monuments, and to cultivate his critical faculties
in the pursuit of the true character of civilization,
the religious, philosophical, and metaphysical
formulæ, of which so many traces lie around him
in the land of his adoption. One of the old
régime, he is not, perhaps, so favourably impressed
with the somewhat violent efforts of the Government to civilize the Egyptians of to-day, as he
might be. A Christian, and a freemason, and a
mathematician, he is a profound believer in the
immense extent and profundity of ancient Egyptian
knowledge. To hear him speak, one would believe
that, in astronomy, the Egyptians of the time of
Pharaoh were, at least, as well versed as the Astronomer Royal. His conversation was, to us all,
singularly interesting, instructive, and novel. Speaking English with the greatest purity and ease (and,
indeed, what language does he not speak?) the
graceful old Armenian was wont to sit for hours
telling us of adventures amongst the Arabs of the
desert, when he was out surveying for the Government in times gone by, or propounding with the
utmost animation his astounding theories concerning the nature of Egyptian monuments, to which
he attributed the deepest significance to be understood only by the instructed.

I was much interested by a visit which I paid my friend one day at his house. It was close to our so-called palace, surrounded by a lofty wall, enclosing a courtyard in front and a large garden in the rear. At the gateway slumbered an ancient janitor, who pointed to the courtyard and called out lazily to one of the servants within, when I asked for his master. Three of the Bey's horses, half-buried in the green pulse which is now given in enormous quantities to cattle to prepare them for the summer droughts, stood at one side of the hall-door in the court. A dromedary, beautifully caparisoned, was in another corner, with its attendant by its head. Some goats, were feeding in another place close to a great Syrian house-dog, and a couple of syces, with their heads covered, were sleeping in the shade of a tree. I passed through the hall to an inner court, where an Arab met me. He led me upstairs to the library, where the venerable Bey sat, at a desk covered with piles of manuscript in inscrutable characters, feeding on books.

About this Arab there is a little story. He is a real child of the desert. When quite a boy, his leg was broken by a fall from a camel. Hekekan Bey set the limb, and won the man's affection so thoroughly that he renounced his nomad life, and

is now a staid domestic in the house. After a
while he went off to the desert, and there married
a woman of his tribe. But nothing would induce
her to abandon her people. Periodically she comes
to Cairo and visits her husband, and after a few
days she returns to the desert. Although full of
gratitude to the Bey for his kindness to her husband, she has never yet let him see her face. She
sits veiled in his presence; and only to the ladies
of his household does she uncover.

I was presented to the wife of the Bey, and to
the wife of his son. The latter speaks French with
fluency; but I could only carry on conversation
with the elder lady by the assistance of the Bey,
who occasionally had to translate some lively in-
vective against his studies and pursuits from Syrian
into English. Coffee was brought in by a young
negress. Slavery is prohibited in Egypt; but, nevertheless, there are in the houses of nearly every
Egyptian, who can afford to pay for them, natives
of Nubia, Abyssinia, and the Soudan, in a condition which may be called voluntary slavery. They
could, we are told, go to the police-stations and
claim their liberty. But they do not. Some
doubting philosophers maintain that the abolition
of slavery is more a form of speech than a fact.

Any way, this black handmaid would not leave
her home for the world. Where, indeed, could
she be so well off as in the house of this considerate master, who never could regard a human
creature as a chattel?

One of the most pleasant excursions during
our stay in Cairo, was to the Museum of Antiquities at Boulak, a suburb on the Nile, which is
regarded as the port of Cairo. Every one who is
interested in Egyptian antiquities has heard, at all
events, of Mariette Bey; but only those who have
seen this admirable collection can appreciate the
immense services he has rendered to antiquaries and
to historians, as only those who have conversed
with him can appreciate his felicity of illustration,
variety of knowledge, and vivacity of expression.

The preparations for the Royal reception received
some impetus or development every day. The
Palace in which their Royal Highnesses and suite
were to lodge became more brilliant with chandeliers and mirrors, and damask hangings. Bed-
steads of solid silver, mirrors set in costly frames,
luxurious ottomans, were poured into the place.
Dozens of gardeners were employed to force the vegetation of some flowers in the patch of sandy soil
between the walls of the Palace and the railing that

separates it from the street. The new theatre, or
circus, was pushed rapidly forward, men toiling
night and day. Fresh coats of paint, and more
gilding, were laid on the boats of the Royal flotilla.
A menagerie arrived. A troop of dancers. Cooks
were summoned from Alexandria. Stores of provisions laid in sufficient, one would think, for a
journey after Livingstone himself.

Every morning the first question asked was, "Any
news of the Prince and Princess?"

Ali Bey, reflecting the Viceregal emotions, became
uneasy. I saw him one morning, in company with
another Bey, sitting in our garden under a tree,
consoling himself with a pipe and coffee whilst the
breakfast was getting ready. "These things," said
he, "are in the hands of God; *He* must know
the Prince has now been 144 hours at sea." It is
not an all-pervading belief in the actual presiding
influence of the Almighty which makes every
Oriental speak in some such fashion; it is a habit
of expression with many. The reprobate cobbler,
who never gives the smallest thought to the in-
junctions of the Koran, has an inscription over
his door from the sacred volume invoking the protection of God, and begins his day's work, or idleness, with a pious ejaculation from the same source.

On 2nd February, returning from an excursion through the town, and a visit to Mr. Ivanovich's remarkable collection of curiosities and antiquities, the Duke received a dispatch from Colonel Stanton, to announce that the Ariadne was just crossing the Bar. The Viceroy was in readiness in his Palace; guards were paraded; all the personages of the Court were in full uniform; cooks were busy preparing the feast, when a later telegram announced it was an error. It was the Psyche, which had been taken for the Ariadne—the Soul for the Flesh—not an uncommon mistake.

" What can have become of the Prince and Princess ?"

A theory was gaining ground that the Prince and Princess had put into Corfu. All the official world in Cairo was in a ferment.

I say " official world," because the circle over which such an event exercises any influence in Egypt is small indeed. Hundreds, nay, thousands of people in Cairo, know nothing about the coming visit. To the apathy of an Oriental race, in all matters except religion, must be added an immense ignorance.

Wednesday, February 3rd. — At last they are coming! There is no doubt about it this time. The Viceroy has received a telegram to report

that the Ariadne is coming in hand - over - hand
towards Alexandria, with Prince and Princess on
board all well.

The Court was once more stirred to its depths.
The Viceroy's household was at once roused to the
fullest activity.

I have already described the palace of Kasr-el-
Nil. It forms but a portion of a series of large
buildings occupied by soldiers. As in most cities,
the Barrack is not far from the Palace. It would
teach the builders of such edifices as some home
barracks a lesson in some respects, if they could see
the amount of light and air, and at the same time
protection from sun and heat, which is afforded
in these barracks, by the arrangement of spacious
balconies and verandahs. The Viceroy has but to
look out of a window, and he will see, on one side,
his soldiers, horse and foot, drilling and manœuvring,
beneath the shade of the trees, in the broad parade-
ground, and, on the other, the boat-covered Nile,
its banks teeming with people and vegetation.

The Zouaves of the Guard, with a troop of Lancers,
were drawn up in the court, facing the palace. The
men appeared too big for the small active white
horses, by which they were standing at ease;
but there was no fault to find in other respects

with their personnel. They wear a red fez, blue
jacket with yellow facings, loose scarlet trousers
and boots, and are armed with a sabre, a lance
with green and purple flag, and a revolver carried
in the holster. Their horses were not well groomed,
and their accoutrements were so ill cleaned as to
draw an exclamation, not laudatory, from our
colonel. Still there is an immense improvement,
according to European notions, in the army,
since I last saw it ten years ago. In the inner
court we found a regiment of infantry drawn up
in columns of companies, which might have been
mistaken at a little distance for the Zouaves of the
Imperial Guard. A closer view would show that
the men were taller, and that they were more stiff
in bearing. A severe - looking captain was busy
adjusting his line, by pressing back protrusive
breasts with the flat of his sword, and he threw
down one objectionable chin with a smart tap
thereon. The officers, but for the fez, would
pass muster for those of the army of our gallant
allies; gold-lace epaulettes, dark-blue frock coats,
small waists, baggy red trousers, patent leather
boots—"a sudden look they would beguile." France
affords the chosen model of the army of the Viceroy and Said Pasha spared no pains and expense

to approximate as closely as he could to his well-beloved beau ideal. The men are still armed with muzzle-loading rifles, with cumbrous sights and bright barrels. Just as with us, so here, the soldier, when he has nothing to do, is best pleased to look at a parade; and the balconies of the spacious quadrangle were filled with the men of another battalion gazing at their fellows.

By the wall of the Palace over the river, where the boats of the Royal flotilla were moored, a crowd of English collected about 4 o'clock. Nor, indeed, were the Americans, who, next to our own people, are the most numerous visitors to Egypt, absent.

The railway sends off a branch to the Palace, and the platform abuts upon the garden, so that a passenger can walk from his carriage to the porch.

Six open carriages, with coachmen, grooms, and outriders, in English liveries, were drawn up in the inner court. As the Viceroy is anxious to patronize both forms of civilization, he has also French fourgons, Normandy horses, French postillions, turned out in the unimpeachable style of M. Fleury's dictatorship under the Second Empire. English horses, carriages, liveries, and servants, for His Highness's personal use, are due, mainly, to the influence of Mr. Smart. A guard of honour, with

standards, was in attendance on the railway platform; knots of wonderfully brilliant staff officers,
of equerries, and aides-de-camp, formed around the
entrance to the Palace; and the great officers of
state, in grande tenue, thronged the hall and the
passages. It was a very pretty scene, full of
colour and light, quickened by the rays of a bright
sun, which did not deprive the air of a keenness
natives and strangers agree in finding rather trying.
The Nile, crisped by a fresh breeze; a regatta-like
fleet of lateen-rigged boats, beating, or running up
and down; the shores lined with palm trees, shaking
their tufted crests in the wind; the irregular outlines of houses, over which appear the tops of the
Pyramids,—these formed the background to the
picture. In the immediate front the colonnades of
the barracks, crowded with soldiers, the lines of
troops under arms, officers, and the gaily-dressed
crowds of ladies, forming a framework, to the front.

On the arrival of our party, we were shown
into the hall, and were summoned to the Viceroy's
presence. He was most anxious to know if everything had been done for the accommodation of his
expected visitors; and after a time, His Highness
led us into the courtyard, and descending the steps
to the Nile, proceeded to conduct us over the

steamers, and the dahabeahs, in which the Royal
party were to make the excursion up the river.

No expense had been spared to render the craft,
inside and out, worthy of those whom the Viceroy
desired to honour. Double - pile carpets to walk
upon ; gilt-legged damask-covered chairs to sit upon ;
luxurious satin couches to recline upon ; mirrors
and brilliant panels to gaze upon ; devices such as
Cleopatra never dreamt of, were prepared for the
comfort of the Prince and Princess. It was puzzling
to decide whether they ought to live on board the
steamer, which was intended for their reception by
day, or on board the dahabeah which was fitted up
for their accommodation by night.

After we had admired everything sufficiently, the
Viceroy returned to the Palace, and I had the
honour of a conversation in his private reception
room. The question of the tribunals mainly
exercised him—that question which rises and meets
one at every turn in Egypt, and of which I have
heard so much since my arrival, and of which most
people know so little. "There are sixteen distinct
nations living in Egypt," said the Viceroy, "and
each nation is independent of my Courts, and
forms a distinct government of its own. They
administer sixteen distinct forms of justice, or, as it

often happens, of injustice. How is a country to be governed, how are my subjects to respect the law, when they see foreigners who have every privilege, whilst they are exempt from every service, enjoying a separate jurisdiction, and, although often opposing each other, agreeing invariably in resistance to the authorities of the country in which they live? I ask nothing more than the formation of a court of European judges, to be appointed by the Great Powers, and to be paid by me, who, sitting with Egyptian judges, shall conduct the trial of offences, according to a code accepted by foreigners and by Egyptians alike."

His Highness evidently feels more deeply upon this matter than upon all or any other affecting Egypt.

" Notwithstanding these tribunals," he proceeded, " Egypt has prospered enormously. But we want colonists. I do not mean labourers, for no European could undergo the toil of the fellah who is obliged to work with his body in the sun, and his feet in the water, day after day, for many months; but intelligent artizans, workmen of various sorts, and skilled mechanics, to whom my Government would offer large advantages, liberal pay, and grants of land. There is no fear of any fanatical opposition to their settlement. We in Egypt are really liberal, and admit the existence of religious differences amongst us. We do not insist upon the profession of any faith as an essential condition of public service. Let a man be honest and capable, and I care not whether he be Armenian, Catholic, or Mussulman ; but before colonization is possible, the question of the Consular tribunals must be settled."

Among the causes assigned by the Viceroy for some little check to the progress of Egypt recently, was the epizootie. Strange to hear the Pharaoh of to-day speaking of the cattle plague in terms that might have been used by the King who would not let the people of Israel go! The murrain which destroyed oxen, camels, sheep, and goats, did not affect the buffalo. A learned Egyptian, in talking of this, insinuated that the cattle of the children of Israel which were exempted from the plague were buffaloes; but there appears to be no warranty for this interpretation of the miracle.

From time to time there came in officers with little scraps of paper to the Viceroy, and, handing them to him with a low reverence, they stood till His Highness had read. These were telegrams reporting the progress of the Prince and Princess. " They are now an hour from Alexandria."—" They

have had lunch."—"They are coming on again."—
" They have passed such a station." As the train
came nearer, the Viceroy was more at ease; for the
fear of accident, little likely as it was, could not
quite be dismissed from his mind.

It was now near 5 o'clock. The last telegram
came in : " The Royal train is approaching Cairo."

" And now I must go and put on my uniform."
He had been wearing that very un-Oriental garb
which is in favour among Oriental personages, the
Quaker-cut single-breasted black frock coat.

In a few moments more we heard the whistle of
the engine, the officers calling the troops to attention in Arabic, the band on the platform striking
up " God save the Queen," which degenerated, or was
elevated, into that quaint air which serves as the
Egyptian national hymn,—wild, martial, and not
unmusical.

The Viceroy passed through the garden from his
Palace, followed by a great crowd of his officers of
state, of the army, of the navy, and of his suite. He
wore a blue frock coat, which was a mass of gold lace
—that rich Egyptian lace, more golden and splendid
than similar manufacture in any place I have been
in—the riband of the Order of the Bath, and star
of diamonds ; a curved scimitar, the hilt of which

seemed a great concrete of diamonds; and the
universal fez, which it is impossible to ornament,
and which mars the effect of uniform, however
magnificent. He arrived on the platform just as
the American carriage, in which were the Prince
and Princess of Wales and their suite, slowly drew
alongside. There was a real cheer from the
English as the Prince and Princess appeared.
The Viceroy, stepping forward, welcomed them in
the most cordial manner, and led the way with
the Princess of Wales upon his arm, the Prince,
who wore his full uniform as a general officer,
being a little in advance.

There was a brief delay inside the Palace ere the
royal travellers reappeared. The Prince of Wales,
coming out first, stepped into a handsome open
carriage with two pair of fine English greys, and
took his seat with his back to the horses. The
Princess of Wales, leaning on the arm of the Viceroy,
was next handed in. Then came a little difficulty.
The Viceroy would insist upon the Prince changing
places. The Prince demurred. But who could resist
the Viceroy in Egypt? And so, after this inter-
change of courtesies, the Royal party drove off, with
the Viceroy facing his guests, who sat in the place
of honour. Tewfik Pasha handed Mrs. Grey into

the next carriage; and the members of the suite
went off in order in the equipages provided for them,
the escort of Lancers having wheeled in after the
first carriage and covered the others with the dust,
which arises on the least provocation in Cairo. The
reception given to their Royal Highnesses was
enthusiastic. Waving handkerchiefs, upraised hats,
and cheers, marked the welcome of the response
of the English and European spectators; but
when the cortége emerged from the Palace
gates, and passed out along the dusty road
towards the new Palace, they met only the
half-scared look of the crowd which, swept away
for a moment by the cavalcade against the walls,
fell out into the streets again, and watched
with a sort of languid curiosity the cloud which
marked the progress of the party towards their
new home—for home it was, so far as the Viceroy
could make it so. There was a guard of honour
at the gates of the Esbekiah Palace, there were
aides-de-camp in waiting, and the crowd of deferen-
tial servants in the hall. The Viceroy led his
guests in, showed them over the rooms, and
then retired. It was almost like living in
public to be in rooms where numberless mirrors
turned one man into a crowd. Four-posters of

I

silver, marble fountains, furniture clotted with
precious metals, immense chandeliers, and gigantic
looking-glasses in prodigious saloons, failed to give
the air which only can be realized in the
palaces of an ancient civilization, where pictures
and objects of art, and books, and a hundred little
evidences of taste, have been accumulated for gene-
rations. One gentleman of the suite had to sleep in
an apartment very like an unfinished metropolitan
church, with a marble floor, and a most costly
fountain of the same material, which in its mercy,
however, had given up playing.

After dinner there was a performance at the
theatre, to which the Prince and Princess and
suite went. The Viceroy received them at the opera-
house, and sat with them during the performance.
It was not a theatre paré, but all the officers
of state were present, and the house was tolerably
well filled. In the pit there was an audience, most
of them wearing the fez, a few the Coptic turban,
others dressed in European fashion; no ladies. The
boxes presented little to distinguish them, but for
the intrusion of the inevitable tarboosh, and the
quaint head-dress and faces of the negro servitors.
Four boxes were set apart for the suite. Directly
opposite the Prince and Princess were two large

boxes, next the stage, in front of which was a
lattice-work, from top to bottom, close and fine—
so close, indeed, as to render it impossible for a
searching opera-glass to pierce its mysteries. These
boxes were not empty, for a certain variation of
colour in the background, and a play of bright hues
inside, showed that the ladies of the harem, nearly
invisible to the outer world, were inside seeing everything. Was it because a gap at the lattice-work
allowed a curious stranger to get a glimpse of a
face within, that an envious mat was suddenly thrust
into it by a black-faced, beardless gentleman in
attendance? It is said that the Viceroy is meditating
a great coup. That lattice-work is some day to
disappear, and the ladies of the court are to sit
unveiled in the presence of the people. But that
day, from all I can hear, must be long distant.
The pieces—"Le Serment d'Horace" and "Contributions Indirectes"—imported from the Palais
Royal, seemed not unsuited to the Cairo audience.
They took the points, laughed at the jokes,
applauded the morceaux when the Viceroy deigned
to nod; and if there was a little broadness
of tone in dialogue and acting, there was
certainly nothing of the wantonness of undress
which we see at home in Christmas panto-

mimes. The theatre is about the size of the
Haymarket. There is a café attached to it, a
restaurant, a bouquetière, bills of the play, and a
saloon where smokers congregate between the acts.
And when you go out into the street, there is the
fellah lying on the bare earth, wrapped in his cloak,
and the wild dogs baying the moon, and the police
calling out the Arab watchwords of the night.

The contrast is striking to a stranger, because
he is looking out for such anomalies. Perhaps
if he were passing through the purlieus of Drury
Lane or Covent Garden after the performance of
play or opera, he would, on examination, discover a
more discordant, significant, and terrible antithesis.
The fellah is not a freeborn Briton with innumerable proud privileges—he is to the manner born,
and can sleep where and how he lists, without
fear of vagrant laws, police cells, or magistrates.
When I was conversing with the Viceroy to-day,
I took the liberty of expressing the regret with
which I saw children of tender years employed
mending the streets of Cairo, in charge of task-
masters. His Highness regretted it too; but he
had his retort.

" You have also in London, my dear, your little
Arabs—vos Arabes de la rue. I have seen them.

I am quite sure they are far more to be pitied
than the little ones of whom you speak, each of
whom has some one to care for it, and who is at
least not a criminal, nor likely to become a pest to
society."

The "smiting" which was in vogue long ago in
the land, is a habit which does not, however, appear
so shocking to us, perhaps, as it must be to other
foreigners. There is much more use of the hand
in England, and among Anglo - Saxon populations
—of the argument called a " blow "—than on the
Continent. To strike one who displeases us is a
natural expedient, only to be restrained by fear or
coerced by law—either of public opinion or of police.
But in Egypt it would seem as if no one dreamt
of resisting the application of it on the part of a
superior, or of obtaining redress. Whoever can hit,
cuff, or kick, does it freely. Sir Anthony Absolute's
mode of ruling a household, and its results, may be
seen any day in the streets. There was a curious
illustration of this rule the other morning near
Shepheard's Hotel. Two men had a dispute over
some matter of sale, and from words one of them,
the larger and stronger, resorted to a sounding box
on the eye of his antagonist. The latter put his
hand to his face, looked round with one glaring

orb at the crowd which had been collected by the controversy, and singling out a laughing donkey-boy, administered to him a tremendous cuff on the side of the head. A few yards away there sat a child of eight or nine years of age against the wall of a house, innocently sucking a piece of sugar-cane. The donkey-boy at once charged him, and kicked him in the ribs. The little fellow looked up, uttered a cry of rage, and seizing a large paving-stone which lay close at hand, flung it—at the donkey-boy?— oh, certainly not! but at a poor street dog, which lay asleep close at hand. The dog immediately went off howling, and no doubt bit a small puppy to ease its mind; and what revenge the puppy took is beyond my knowledge, but no doubt he did something vindictive in his turn.

February 4th.—A bright sun and cold wind. The Royal party were up early, and drove in carriages through the bazaar to the Citadel, to see the departure of the pilgrims with the Holy Carpet to Mecca.

Of the thousands of Europeans who visit Cairo, there are few who have the fortune to behold the spectacle, which may be described in many books to me unknown, but which can never be adequately described in any book at all. The sight is called

"the departure of the Pilgrims for Mecca." That
is a misnomer. It is in reality a procession of
sheiks and holy men and the sacred Mahmal and
Kisweh, escorted by irregular cavalry and guns,
which leaves the city to go out to the real pilgrims
encamped on the plain outside Cairo. The Mahmal
is a wooden canopy covered with gold brocade and
silk, which is symbolical of the litter of Sheger-
ed-Deen, the wife of the Sultan Es-Saleh-Nebn-
ed-Deen, on her journey to Mecca. The Kisweh
is the covering which is put over the Raabeh,
in the Temple at Mecca. Several days ago the
pilgrims set out from Cairo, and encamped on the
Abbasaya. What rites and ceremonies they may
have been since performing, inside and out, I know
not ; but last night all sightseers were warned that
the ceremonial was to come off soon after 9 o'clock.
At that hour the Viceroy's carriages were in waiting
at the Prince's Palace, and a guard of honour, with
a trumpet band, was drawn up in the open space
between the building and the street. There were
very few people attracted by the show of horses and
guards; but the crowds which gathered in the narrow
streets through which the procession was to pass,
gave proof of the enormous population of this
swarming city. The Prince, Princess, and suite,

attended by the Duke of Sutherland and his party, set out about 10 o'clock, and drove to the open space beneath the Citadel, famous as the scene of the demolition of the Mamelukes by Mehemet Ali. They were preceded by horsemen, and by the running footmen who are the heralds of every carriage in Cairo—by night pillars of fire; by day bounding with feet that never tire before the horses, crying out incessantly in Arabic, freely translated, "Mind your toes!" or, "Look out, there!" To a man of cruel or arbitrary disposition the office must be enviable, for it gives, apparently, a right to the bearer to smite whatever and whomever he pleases. The number of unoffending men, and camels, and asses punished in Cairo every day by smart raps of a long cane, for doing nothing at all! but being alive, by these officials, must amount to many hundreds; and they all bear it with equal mind and body. The route from the Prince's Palace to the Citadel lies through a part of the town which is, perhaps, the most striking and interesting of all Cairo. Familiar as the city is to European travellers, there is about its streets an ingredient of what may be understood, though not defined, by the word "Orientalism," which is ever suggesting new ideas, or reviving old ones. A good deal of

interest, no doubt, is due to the belief which unconsciously underlies the spectator's wonder that
he is looking at people who are in thought, dress,
and habits very much what they were many centuries
ago, and who, all alive, are yet as dead as if
they were mummified for all the purposes of this
progressive, practical, prosaical half-century. The
streets wind in and out at discretion, through a
mass of houses, mosques, and bazaars, very much
as mites march through a cheese. The word
"street" gives no conception of the lane which
scarcely ever yields a view of 100 yards in front or
behind, and which at times seems to end abruptly
in the cordial greeting of two houses at opposite
sides. There is quite enough to detain the stranger
for a pleasant ten minutes—for every ten paces if
he likes — to loiter and be jostled by asses and
shoved aside by the crowd, or scared by growling,
fierce-toothed camels. There are the shops, with
their varied stores and still more varied owners
and customers, the incorrigible, persecuting, stick-
disregarding donkey-boys, who never desist from
importunate solicitation to mount "Champagne
Charley," "Lord John Russell," "Palmerston," or
some other famous quadruped with long ears and
indomitable back-bone. Over the shops rises the

lattice-windowed frontage of the houses, sometimes
projecting from the drawing-room floor upwards on
frail beams, sometimes coyly retiring, seldom guilty
of a real perpendicular. While all below is life,
and noise, and activity, from the first floor upwards
there is silence in the house. Now and then a
child may be caught sight of at the lattice, or a
draped face gleams out of a pair of inquiring eyes
on the world below; but mostly there is a blank
in the Egyptian quarter. To-day this was changed,
and all womankind was enjoying its rare holyday,
and enjoying it more, perhaps, too, than its sister-
hood in England would if it were all going off to
the poll, headed by Miss Becker and Mr. Mill, to
record its vote for some political Apollo Belvedere.
The women, clad in sweeping robes, which in their
combination form such tempting, yet distracting
subjects, for the artist who loves to paint masses of
coloured drapery, sat with their children chattering
in every safe recess in the streets. They gazed out
of the latticed windows, through the sluice-like open
traps, and through the open casements, crowded
the flat roofs, swarmed on the mosque-tops, and
clustered in the doorways. If eyes can be an
index to the character of the rest of the face, many
of the ladies must have been very beautiful; but

some showed the ravages of ophthalmia, which the
artifice of blackened eyebrows only made more
evident. The men and boys of the different nations
and faiths which have their representatives here
—Arabs, Jews, Copts, Syrians, Egyptians, Turks,
Franks, Nubians, Albanians, Anatolians, Greeks,
Persians, Circassians, "barbarians," and dwellers in
partibus infidelium, dressed each after his kind, lined
the streets and sat in the bazaar shops, and on the
shifting kaleidoscopic multitude, over which the fine
dust rose from the tread of many feet, there came
down, through the chinks in the latticed screen
which covers in the street, rays of sunshine which
produced the most striking and charming effects.
Through this scene imagine camels plodding along
with ponderous loads of green vetches, asses hidden
under mounds of vegetables and tares for fodder,
or laden with important portions of a small
family; horses and ponies, and their riders; mules
and dromedaries, with their turbaned or veiled
burdens; and then, pressing through the throng,
an advance guard of native outriders, followed by
a host of running footmen, in front of an open
carriage with prancing horses, driven by an unmis-
takable British coachman,—and fancy the expression
of delight and surprise on the fair face, dear to so

many millions of people in islands far away. Now
and then, when a refractory camel blocked the path,
or a dog gave warning of some small personal grief,
or the carriage was caught at a narrow corner by
stray dromedaries with far-extending platforms on
their backs, the Princess evinced a transient
anxiety. The good humour of the people, their
civility and temper, as carriage after carriage
came crushing and squeezing them out of the
roadway into shop-fronts and side lanes — nay,
even the placidity of holy men and dervishes of
renown, whose donkeys and camels were cuffed, and
whose venerable persons were shoved unceremoni-
ously aside—were much to be commended. At last
the cortége emerged into the open space below the
Citadel. Here, round the sides of a large extent of
cleared ground, were drawn up the troops of the
line, Lancers and Zouaves of the Guard, and the
400 irregular cavalry which were to guard the
pilgrims and escort the treasure annually sent to
the sheiks of the Arab tribes and to Mecca. Behind
this line were congregated crowds of people. They
were on the citadel walls, on the flat roofs, and on
the sides of the mosques, wherever they could see;
and above them all shone a bright sun in a sky
of heavenly blue. As the Prince and Princess of

Wales came in sight, the troops presented arms
along the lines, the irregular cavalry tapped their
little saucer-like drums, and the bands saluted
with the Zouave "As tu vu la casquette, &c., de
Père Bugeaud," now familiar to so many Britishers.
The carriages drove up to a raised dais, draped
with curtains of scarlet and gold, and provided
with chairs, where the Viceroy's eldest son, Tewfik
Pasha, surrounded by the officers of State in full
uniform, received them.   Seats were provided for
the Consular body and their friends and the principal
residents and visitors.   Indeed, a white face, a bad
hat and shabby travelling clothes, seem to be a
passport here to every place.   The Prince made the
acquaintance of the little Pasha, the Viceroy's
youngest son, who was beautiful in scarlet stockings,
scarlet and gold knickerbockers, and a cream-coloured
jacket slashed with gold lace.   The superior officers,
mounted on their richly caparisoned Arabs, sat in
front of the dais.   After a time the head of the procession emerged from under an archway at the
opposite side of the esplanade.   It was preceded
by men with sticks to keep away the crowd, who
certainly "kept their sticks going" in a way which
would astonish a line of beaters in a home covert.
Then came men and boys chanting and shouting

in front of the camels, one of which bore the
Mahmal. Some sustained lofty saddles and saddle
bags, decorated with orange branches and short flag-
staffs with banners; others carried holy hadjees or
sheiks. One was honoured by a peculiar, if not
agreeable load—a very sainted personage, whose
great merit it was and is, to keep turning his
head round on his neck, as if it were fixed on
a universal joint, all the way to Mecca. This man,
very crass and unctuous, was bare headed; his
grizzled, dirty-looking locks, divided in the centre,
being his only covering from the blazing sun of
Arabia. His body was stripped down to the
waist, and gave evidence that, in spite of his head
turnings, the holy man put on flesh wonderfully.
His eyelids were half closed, his fat face had an
utter want of expression, quite suitable to the head
it belonged to, which went round and round at
every jog of the much more intelligent-looking camel
which he bestrode. Year after year this saint has
turned his empty head, and seems none the worse
—nay, all the better for it; though thousands of his
fellow-pilgrims, who do not turn their heads, perish
miserably in the pilgrimage. When the holy camel
of the Kisweh came to the dais, the Pasha was
handed one of the holy cords, and kissed it, and

then the chief sheik took it and kissed it, and
the procession of camels, of singing men and
shouting boys, defiled twice in a circle in front
of the dais, while the guns of the citadel thundered
out a salute, and then marched away towards
the city to take part in the greater procession.
Now, dashing at full speed from the end of
the esplanade, came a solitary horseman holding
a long quivering lance, which he poised across
his saddle, and now and then thrust right
and left. This was the leader of the irregular
horsemen, "the Lord of the Land," a great chief
in Egypt this day. He threw his horse on his
haunches with a cruel bit, wheeled round, wielding
but not throwing his lance, and careless of the
multitude, which now broke into the enclosed space
and pressed round the dais. It is the habit to
give money annually at this festival, and frightful
fighting and confusion ensued; but in consideration
for the Princess it was not observed. The results
of a scramble might be guessed from the scene
which occurred when the police and the cavalry had
to clear the way through the " people " in a way
which would have done Superintendent Walker good
to see. Sticks? I should think so. Bludgeons!
Whips! It rained blows on the heads and shoulders

of King Mob, who has a very hard time of it. How no skull was cracked was a marvel to those who opine the Egyptian cranium is not solid. But no corpses were left on the ground, and the carriages drove off to see the procession. The route lay now through narrow lanes and streets in which there was scarcely a sign of life. Here and there a workman, more industrious or less religious than his fellows, sat cross-legged beside a heap of cakes or sweetmeats, and a few inhabitants wondering at the sight of the passing carriages. After a time, however, we came out into the crowded thoroughfare, and, with greater difficulty than before, the little cortége made its way through the people to the house provided for the accommodation of the Prince and Princess. Passing through an open porte-cochère, where the Prince and Princess were received by gentlemen in waiting, the party ascended a steep staircase which led to two large rooms furnished with carpets and divans, the open windows of which looked on the street. Far as the eye could reach, up and down, and on either side, it was crowded in the same way as the part of the city which I have already tried to describe.

Pipes and coffee were brought in by the servants, and unaccustomed lips made some slight experi-

ment on the massive amber mouthpieces. But a
hum and bustle in the crowd summoned the party
to the windows. Round a turn in the street there
came in view an irregular multitude, preceded by
horsemen tapping small saucer-like drums, and by
men on foot with sticks and balls slung to cords
like those used by jugglers at home, who cleared the
way for a very motley, picturesque, and eccentric
procession of footmen, marching abreast—four, or
five, or six in front. The turbans worn by each
section of orthodox sects were of the same colour.
Banners—green, and white, and yellow, inscribed
with texts from the Koran—every few yards, were
borne in pairs, suspended from lofty poles with
gilt tops. There were many hundreds of these banners, which are stored up carefully by the sheiks
when the ceremony is over. Between the banner-
bearers came men and boys uttering shrill cries,
or chanting in unison, with a certain sort of mono-
tonous sweetness, verses from the Koran. Others
marched to the sound of flageolets and drums. Occasionally there appeared some singular, if not revolt-
ing, object. Now men, stripped to the waist, holding, by hilt and point, a curved sword, which they
pressed against their naked stomachs. The edges
were blunt. But the point was not always so, since

K

an indiscreet sabreur who forgot that fact cut
his fingers, to his evident discomfiture. Now, men
holding by the tail writhing serpents, three or four
feet long, which darted out their forked tongues
at the bare legs of the shrinking crowd. Anon, it
was a shirtless man, who leapt about, brandishing
two unsheathed swords across his neck and belly.
Now a group of boys slinging balls of metal, like
cup and ball, or burning incense in braziers. Again
venerable men on asses and mules, inveterate old
pilgrims in long-robed dresses, descendants of the
Prophet, in green turbans. Men with big drums,
cripples and mendicants who live on piety and
exceeding uncleanliness of person, men singing
and beating cymbals, and tambourines. The
strains of martial music announced the approach
of the Egyptian troops. They were preceded
by the officer in command and his staff, well
mounted, and by a picturesque avant-garde of
pioneers, with bearskins like those of the Old Guard,
white leather aprons, and great axes en règle.
The first battalion which marched past were tall,
well-set-up, fine young men, dressed in fez, light
blue jackets, vests with yellow facings, scarlet
trousers and gaiters à la Zouave — whose uniform
the Egyptians say was borrowed from their army.

They kept time to a man, and, altogether, looked
as if they could meet any troops that could be
brought against them on equal terms, if officered
properly. Breechloaders are not come to them
yet.

Three battalions, each headed by its trumpets
playing the Zouave pas, went by, and after them
the cavalry, with green and purple-flagged lances,
swords, and pistols, headed by a band which was
described by a young gentleman fresh from England
as "a caution to rattlesnakes." Their horses, full of
life, were small, active, unshod, ill-cleaned. Their
dress, a fez, blue jackets and yellow facings, yellow-
striped blue vest, and red trousers. Next came
the General of Cairo, with a very showy staff, in
front of whom rode a few horsemen with breech-
loading revolving carbines. Another detachment of
infantry followed. And then the holy camels and
the man with the revolving head went by, and after
them, flowed on a crowd with banners and devices
and dervishes, just like the first. Then the irregular
cavalry, beating their tom-toms, mounted on all
sorts of horses, armed with many kinds of weapons,
having pistols stuck everywhere over them, guns
of all kinds in their hands and slung over their
backs, and pendant from their saddles. A specimen

of every firearm made for the last 150 years could
assuredly have been collected from among their
armament. Their music was terrible, and the wild
troopers must have been a thorn in the flesh to
small boys, as it was their sport to pluck off the
fezzes and skull caps of the unwary, and fling them
among the crowd or under the hoofs of their
shoeless horses. Next, as the end of all things, a
field battery of six rifled bronze guns, with two
mules to each gun, followed by another tumultuous
crowd and mounted men; and at last the tail of
the procession, which if long drawn out was by no
means always linked sweetness, disappeared round
an angle of the street, which was at once filled by
the people who had previously lined it. After the
procession passed, the Prince and Princess returned
to the Palace; and later in the day the Princess
drove out quietly with Mrs. Grey through the
bazaar, and did a little original shopping. The
Prince drove to the Viceregal Palace, visited the
Viceroy, and had pipes and coffee, and thence went
to the Nile, to inspect the Alexandra dahabeah
and the flotilla prepared for the Royal party.

In the course of the afternoon, and somewhat
to the discomfiture of refined courtiers, who do not
think donkey riding compatible with dignity, some

of the party proceeded in a long train through
the bazaars in that fashion, to the great delight
of the donkey boys, who soon learned the rank
of the distinguished personages who had honoured
them with their patronage.

A visit to the Duke of Sutherland's Palace was
included in the excursion by the Prince and Princess
and suite, and there again pipes and coffee were for
the third time presented to them. In the evening
" La Grande Duchesse " was represented for the first
time in Cairo, and was exceedingly appreciated by
the native part of the audience.

February 5th.—At 12 o'clock the Royal party,
with the Duke of Sutherland and friends, visited

the New Palace of the Viceroy at Gizeh, on the left bank of the Nile.

The object of building a new palace must be best known to him who is master of so many. Here, certainly, he has succeeded in obtaining one of the most beautiful residences that king or emperor can desire. The palace is not yet finished, but has already cost more than £250,000. It is not alone sumptuous halls, immense saloons, decorated in the most exquisite manner in imitation of the Alhambra, nor gorgeous mirrors, nor chandeliers, nor furniture covered with beaten gold that renders it so. The floors of the rooms are composed of different coloured marbles. The taste and fancy of Europe have been lavished on the architecture of the Moor. It stands in the midst of gardens, set in by a framework of date-palms; one wanders through groves of exotics, and alleys bordered by oriental plants, watered continuously by noble fountains. There is a menagerie of wild beasts close at hand, and cranes, and saruses, and flamingoes stalk about the avenues.

Outside there is a kiosk and a harem, corresponding in richness and finish with the main building. The party proceeded through the bazaar, and thence went to see performances of the dancing dervishes.

Here is one of the holy men! He does not dance, but spins round like a humming-top. There are some twenty of them, tapering away from the tallest who is in the centre, and the whirling of each has an orbit, so that every man slowly describes an ellipse. There is supposed by the savans to be some astronomical truth typified in the dance—the motions of the

sun and planets—but the dervishes did not look at all philosophical, and they certainly were not indifferent to terrestrial matters in the way of backsheesh. The crowd regarded the performance without enthusiasm; but I never saw a bishop of any church who looked at all equal to doing the like of it.

The Princess of Wales and Mrs. Grey, in the afternoon, visited the harem of the Viceroy, where they were received by the Valideh, and were pre-

sented to the ladies of the establishment. The
Princess was the object of great attention on the part
of the ladies during the three hours she remained
there, and returned with many pleasant anecdotes.

A donkey ride along the Schoubra Road helped
to get over a portion of the day; and after dinner
the Royal party went to the theatre, where "La
Belle Hélène" was performed. Menelaus was
certainly to be congratulated on the departure of
his faithless spouse, and I am sure Paris bounded
nimbly out of his bark when the curtain fell.

There is little else to be done in the evening in
Cairo. There are no parties or balls; no receptions
which ladies can attend. The Viceroy, however,
being desirous of showing His Royal Highness an
exhibition of the native dancing and singing, with
which the upper classes are entertained in their own
houses, invited him and his suite to the Kasr-el-
Nil after the play.

We had the opportunity of hearing the Cairo
Grisi, a woman of about forty years of age, neither
fat, nor fair to look upon, who sang at fitful
intervals, to the accompaniment of six chosen
musicians. The music put one much in mind of
that in Upper India. The lady's voice was somewhat cracked; but there were quaint odd notes, in

which still lingered traces of the melody which she
possessed in her youth.   Her principal attraction
now, however, is said to be her wit and liveliness.
She talked to the Viceroy without the smallest
gêne; and in a keen encounter of wit between
her and Sir Samuel Baker in Arabic, it was said
by proficients that the Englishman had the worst
of it. There were six women dancers, who performed singly and in pairs.

The Egyptian dance has often been described.
Some varieties of it, executed by these ladies, were
stated—on what authority I know not—to date
from the time of the Pharaohs. Others were content
with putting them down roughly at 2,000 years old;
to suit the antiquity of the performances, the ladies,
with two exceptions, were ancient and mummified.

The gentlemen were seated on divans round the
room, and it was considered a mark of attention on
the part of the Almeah, or Dancing Girl, to select
some particular person whom she fancied to be
worthy of her consideration, and to dance specially
before him.

It was rather a relief, on the whole, when the
Viceroy led the way with the Prince down to
supper, from which we did not return to Cairo
till half-past 2 in the morning.

CHAPTER VI.

February 6th.—The entertainment given by the
Viceroy last night led to rather a late breakfast; but
the Royal party were ready to start at an earlier
hour than we expected. At 12 o'clock the Prince
of Wales and his suite drove to the Citadel to visit
the Viceroy's son, where they had pipes and coffee.

It is the etiquette of the East, that one who is
visited by a great personage, should immediately
return the compliment; and no sooner had the
Prince got back to his palace, than the Pasha
made his appearance with his suite, and paid his
parting compliments to His Royal Highness; for
this was the day of the departure of the two
parties from Cairo.

There were beys, and aides, and cavasses flying
about in all directions; and a gathering of many
officials round the doors of the Prince's palace.
There is always a little bustle attendant on the
starting of a large party; and our small palace was
pretty lively from 10 till 1 o'clock, when all the
boxes, portmanteaus, bags, and gun-cases were safely
loaded on trucks and sent down to Kasr - el - Nil,
where the steamers were moored. The Duke of
Sutherland and party went to the railway station to
meet Lord Albert Gower and Sir H. Pelly, who were
coming from Alexandria, quite unconscious of their
fate. They were touring about and had telegraphed
to announce their arrival at Alexandria; and it was
resolved that they should be taken up the Nile, the
very moment they arrived. It is seldom a man is
called on to execute such a sudden journey in con-
tinuation of a route which was intended to end for
the time at a railway terminus.

Soon after 1.30 o'clock the Prince and the Princess,
in plain travelling clothes, suited to the climate, started
in an open carriage, the suite following in others, and
drove at a rapid rate to Kasr-el-Nil. There were
very few of the natives who appeared to know or
to care for their departure. Not even a scurry of
Egyptian outriders, or gentlemen in waiting in

their peculiar costume — black jacket, embroidered
vest, with sash, black knickerbockers, black embroidered leggings—and a guard of cavasses riding
at full speed, and warning all to get out of the
way, created much excitement among the people;
and when the cortége got out on the mound-marked
road, leading through fields of sugar-cane and tares, to

the bank of the river, the peasants, working at their
leisure, in the fields, and the fellah men and women,
scarcely raised their heads to give a speculating
glance at the cloud of dust which whirled along the
causeway. At the entrance to the castle-yard, the
guard turned out in their white summer fatigue-
jackets, knickerbockers, and gaiters, and saluted.

The Palace itself was all silent; the jalousies closed
as if the Viceroy did not like to see his guests'
departure; and there were not fifty people in all,
including the stray soldiery in the court at the
Nile wall, to see the start of the flotilla. The Duke
of Sutherland and his party were already on board
The Ornament of Two Seas.

The Prince and Princess and Mrs. Grey occupied
the Alexandra dahabeah, which was towed by the
Royal steamer. There was also a kitchen steamer
attached to it.

Lieut.-Col. Teesdale, Captain Ellis, Mr. Montagu,
Dr. Minter, Lord Carington, Sir Samuel Baker,
Prince Louis of Battenberg, and Mr. Brierly were
accommodated on board the steamer, in which the
Royal party daily assembled for breakfast and
dinner.

Another steamer was provided for Mourad Pasha
and Colonel Stanton, on board of which Major
Alison, who belonged to the Duke of Sutherland's
party, was provided with a berth. Mr. Fowler
and Professor Owen, who had been invited by the
Duke to accompany him, finding that the room on
board the fourth steamer was rather limited, were
wont to take refuge in the evening on board Colonel
Stanton's boat.

A lighter, containing stores, was towed by the kitchen steamer; another lighter, with four horses, and a riding-donkey for the Princess, was towed by the steamer assigned to Colonel Stanton.

His Royal Highness has got Mr. Baker, a clever naturalist and taxidermist, on board. His punt is well adapted for the sport to be had on the river, and is in charge of Webster, who was with Lord Londesborough on the Nile some years ago, when he made up his famous tale of 10,000 head of birds in one season.

Talk of the doings of djins and afreets! What did they know of champagne and soda-water and French patés? One of them could not have got a bottle of brandy to save his life—the genii who lived in the vessel in the sea surely could not have obtained his freedom had it depended on producing a flask of Curaçao. Well, on board the store boat, for fear of one going athirst on the voyage, there was, it is said, a supply of 3,000 bottles of champagne, 20,000 bottles of soda-water, 4,000 bottles of claret; and so on as to sherry, and ale, and liqueurs of all sorts.

About 2 o'clock the start was effected, and a very pretty sight it was. First the Prince's steamer moved off, with the Royal Standard and Ottoman flag flying; next the Alexandra dahabeah, or sleeping-boat;

then, the steamer on board of which were Colonel
Stanton, Professor Owen, Mr. Fowler, and Major
Alison; next the cooking steamer; then the Duke of
Sutherland's steamer, and a boat serving as a tender
to the little flotilla, each in turn towing a barge
full of provisions. There was a good deal of shouting; but on the whole not much to complain of.
I am not going to try my hand at a Nile picture.
Mr. Murray, by the aid of Sir Gardner Wilkinson,
has indicated every object of interest on the banks
of the river after leaving Boulak. The photographer
and the colourist (if a painter submits to be so
called) must do the rest; for it is but a useless repetition of words, conveying no just impression to the
mind of the reader, to write of mosques and palaces
and ruins on the banks; of waving date-palms; of
water-wheels at work; of green fields; of fellah
women, with covered heads and bodies and bare legs,
by the river side; of men, only to be distinguished
from women by their turbaned heads; of minarets
in the distance; of lateen-rigged boats, with stumpy
masts and enormous yards; of Arab crews and
cargoes—mounds of chopped straw piled on deck,
heaps of water-jars, coops of noisy fowl, gobbling
turkey-cocks; one might go on enumerating such
things for ever, as we paddle up the great water-way

which is the artery of life and commerce for five millions of people clustered along its course.

The last sight of interest was the great mosque of Sultan Hassan, in Cairo—far away—which came in view at a bend of the river, and shone out gloriously in the rays of the setting sun, giving fair reason to question the judgment of the critics who have complained of the slenderness of the two graceful minarets, which, to our eyes, were exquisite in proportion and effect.

The worst of a steamboat, in one respect, is, that it always enables one to go on,—and on he goes accordingly; whereas, in the sailing vessel, odious as delays may be, there is much involuntary sight-seeing to be done when the wind is foul. No doubt we passed many interesting places — the quarries, for example, whence, for thousands of years, magnesian limestone has been cut for monuments, palaces, and cities, and where a man may wander in the galleries hewn into the mountain for a day without coming to an end of them. The Nile is so low that the various layers of successive years' inundations may be traced, like strata in rocks.

"The proper study of mankind is man," particularly if you have good lorgnettes and telescopes.

I would be ashamed to say how much more we were
interested in watching the progress of the Royal
yacht, and in observing those on board of her, than
in scrutinizing the sites of famous places on both
sides of the river above Cairo. "There is the
Princess! You can just see her in the saloon on
deck!" The mounds of old Babylon, and the
mosque built over the "Footprint of the Prophet,"
were on one side; on our right towered the Pyramids
of Gizeh, and as the steamers cleft their way
against the turbid stream, there rose in sight the
Pyramids of Abooseer, Sakkara, and Dashoor: but
they could be seen at any time, whilst it was not so
certain when we could get a glimpse of the Prince
on the Nile, in the abandon of shooting-jacket,
knickerbockers, and felt hat. If such were the feelings of the party, what might not be pardoned to
Mr. Cook's Tourists, who were in full cry up the
river after the Prince and Princess? Some of our
companions had come from Brindisi with the British
caravan, and gave accounts which did not tend to
make us desire a closer acquaintance. Respectable
people—worthy—intelligent—whatever you please;
but all thrown off their balances by the prospect of
running the Prince and Princess of Wales to earth in
a Pyramid, of driving them to bay in the Desert, of

hunting them into the recesses of a ruin—enraptured
at the idea of being able possibly to deliver " an
address " in the temple of Karnak, or of gazing at
their ease on the Royal couple, enclosed in their
toils on the Island of Philæ. The quarries of **El
Mahsarah** and **Toora**, worked twenty centuries and
more before the Christian era, which furnished the
materials of the Gizeh pyramids, and the Temples
of Thebes and Memphis, were on our left hand, and
we were obliged to take, on hearsay, that there were,
in the galleries of these mothers of many cities,
marks, as legible as if they were cut yesterday, of
the kings who ordered the works. Far away over
the opposite bank, you can note the mounds of rubbish which are all that remain of what was once
" imperial Memphis." " I can see the Prince! he
is just forward there, speaking to Baker!" There
is certainly some subtle sort of pleasure in looking
at Royalty through a powerful glass. You are a
long way off, and you cannot be considered intru-
sive. And so you stare—I beg your pardon, sir, or
madam, if I wrong you!—very much with the sort
of satisfaction a stalker experiences, at a calm, con-
templative, all-over look from the top of some heathery
knoll at an Imperial or Royal head, unconscious of
the inspection. We pass the sulphur springs of

Helwan, where it is conjectured Amenophis sent
lepers and other incurables to live apart from the
rest of Egypt. Manetho says he did the thing,
but does not mention the name of the place—that
is, Sir Gardner Wilkinson declares Manetho makes
the statement. I confess I have not consulted
the passage in which the extract from Manetho is
recorded, and that I am as unlearned respecting
Manetho as was the worthy gentleman in the "Vicar
of Wakefield," who quoted him and Sanconiathon.
But recent researches have enhanced the value of the
ancient priest's chronicles, and Egyptologists bless the
fortunate chance which, in the writings of another,
saved his lists from destruction. Just now, as mound
after mound denote the graves in which whole cities
lie buried—Aphroditopolis, the city of Acanthus, the
temple of Osiris—there is an alarm "The tourists
are coming!"

A cloud of smoke rises from a steamer astern,
but after a time it is made out that she is a local
merchant craft bound to one of the sugar factories,
and peace of mind is restored. The signal for
dinner flies along the line, and Ali Risa, who pre-
sides, is proudly conscious that there is no difference
made in the menu by the change of scene, and
that our Spanish cook and Italian domestics, trans-

ferred from the palace, are resolved to make The
Ornament of the Two Seas a rival of the dwelling
on the Schoubra Road.

Our steamer does not present much to talk about.
There is the usual grave, keen-eyed, dark-faced old
Arab reis, in white turban and flowing robes, at the
wheel—a handsome old fellow, who is relieved by
another—his very ditto, only a shade graver, and
better - looking ;   our captain, a blue-eyed, rather
feeble-faced Turk, who is afraid " to go ahead," and
has not quite recovered the effect of the Ramadan ;
the crew of marines, in greyish coats, blue trousers,
and fez, all the worse for wear, taking measure of
the new-comers ; in the bow, the butchers arraying
the fore-rigging with carcases of poultry and sheep ;
astern, our excellent Italian servants, our old staff
at the Palace, cheerfully chatting as they prepare
for il pranso. Some of our good sailors, taking in
turn a flat cushion on the quarter-deck, say their
prayers, and shame us all by their open-air courage
of devotion. The evening became cold by the
time we had got twenty miles up the river, and
our steamer, faster and lighter than the Prince's
boat, which was, moreover, towing the dahabeah,
went on ahead, and lost sight of the flotilla in
a bend of the river. The Prince ran aground soon

after we left him, and others did the same, so
that they made very slow work of it. At dusk,
we sidled up to the bank of the river on the
right, near a village called Kafr (or "village")
Iabt, or Ayabt. The Prince's boat, and attendant
steamers, came up and clawed the bank alongside
later in the evening. It is easy work to moor
a vessel, as a stake driven into the soft rich
earth is sufficient to hold the warp of a large
ship. A plank is thrown out to the steep bank,
and steps are cut up to the top by the sailors.
At each plank sits or stands a swarthy Egyptian,
holding a pole, atop of which is an iron frame-work
holding a mass of blazing pine and coals, which
throws a bright light on the landing-place, and
lights up the hulls and white funnels of the
vessels and the dusky waters. The line of these
beacons, and the lanterns slung from the mizen-
rigging, formed an effective illumination, but did
not attract the natives out of the mud-heaps
called villages. After dinner, the party were invited
to go on board the Prince's boat, and scrambled
along the bank to the gangway. If there were any
wandering fellahs about, they must have heard the
tinkle of the piano, touched by a fair and practised
hand, and the refrain of songs, and clamour of

choruses, not unfamiliar in England. What the theories of the hypothetical auditors may have been respecting the strains, who can determine?

But I can assure you, when deep called unto deep —when Alister, beating the deck proudly with his foot, made the date groves resonant with " the sweetest notes ear ever heard " (on the pipes, be it understood), and summoned Peter Robertson to generous, but not successful, emulation, on bag and slender reed—when " Farewell to Lochaber " was borne on the evening air from The Ornament of the Two Seas to be re-echoed from the Prince's ship by eldrich slogan—they must have been stout aborigines who stood unmoved, and the feelings of the guardians of our watch-fires on the bank must have been too deep for words. It is no fault of Peter Robertson that he cannot play the pipes as well as Alister, who has a gift that way, and who was born past master in the fearful and mystic art; for he can touch heart and feet, and set both beating together. But Peter is great in the forest and on the " hull," and it is not given to all to excel on the bagpipes and in the chase. By persevering efforts, which the fellahs and I would prefer to have developed at first in some lonely glen, rather than in our immediate vicinity, he may dominate the tender and

pathetical power of the instrument, from which now
rush martial sounds and war's alarms, as though
Æolus had loosed his windy caverns in anger.
Hamed, Hadji Ali, Achmet Captan, Ali Captan, the
Reis—in the plural; I cannot say Reises—and the
crews, agreed that it was capital music altogether,
and that they had never heard the like of it
before.

We shook down pretty comfortably at night.
There is a cabin astern, with a long sofa on
both sides, which gave resting-place to the Duke
and Colonel Marshall. Two small cabins, between
it and the dining saloon, were occupied by the
Marquis of Stafford and myself. The cushions
round the dining saloon afforded sumptuous beds
for Lord Albert Gower and Sir Henry Pelly, and
at the end of the companion ladder outside Mr.
Sumner held high state in the largest cabin, which
was only unfortunate in its vicinity to the boilers
and to the bath-room—an apartment with a zinc
hip bath, which, filled with Nile water, was in
much request, and the object of considerable in-
trigue, foul play, and manœuvring before breakfast.

Sunday, February 7th.—The morning was dull
and the sun overcast—the wind cold for the country
and the time of year. The fleet got under weigh

soon after daybreak, and pressed on against the current of the Nile, now hugging one shore—again creeping to the other—now keeping the middle, as the skippers were warned by the cries of the watchmen on the banks, or by the advice of the native boats. The channel is for ever shifting. To provide as far as possible against our running aground, the Viceroy sent up instructions six weeks ago to have the course of the river closely observed; and ever since, day and night, the people have been watching and waiting for us. Groups of horsemen, here—men in boats, there—voices sounding from bank to bank, exchange the words of council with our captain and the Arab reis at every turn.

The character of the scenery has a certain monotony, of which we do not tire. There are the Pyramids of Lisht; there is the False Pyramid. There a mass of rock as like a Pyramid as if Nature were trying to emulate the grand freaks of these great builders. There are groups of women, by the water's edge, with their heads covered, in dark blue robes, and legs naked to the knee, filling the huge jars, which they bear gracefully on their heads, or crouching down to plash their limbs — along the banks men riding

—villages—date trees—gliding sails—the railway
and the telegraph posts.

The river is covered with boats, the crews of each
a study for a painter; their cargoes a wonder; their
ability to float at all—not to mention their speed—

something to be surprised at, for they need a luteing
of mud and chopped straw round the hatchway to
keep out the water. After a run of three hours,
the Prince's steamer stopped—at first voluntarily—
to get breakfast from the kitchen boat, and next
involuntarily on a sand-bank. Our boat went on
ahead. We passed an ancient Coptic convent—
Dehra Mahmed; a deserted Christian village; the
lone tomb of a holy man, solitary on the sand,
guarded by a few palm trees; another tomb of a
sainted lady, whose memory is held in veneration
by devout Mahometans, who come in pilgrimage
to the shrine — another of her daughter, who is
also of blessed memory. Small dust storms
whirl round and round on shore. The steamer
shoots by El Mazabyeah-o-Bitashar, observed of
many detached gatherings of men apart and
women apart on the banks. We look for crocodiles with the eye of credulity, but Hamed says
there are none to be seen now much below Assouan,
and that as long as the wind is cold they stay in
the river, and do not visit the banks. The hippopotamus is not met with below Berbeh, which is
north of Khartoum. Hamed says a thousand years
ago it was found as low—as far north—as we are
now; I believe Hamed in any matter relating to

hippopotami, even to the extent of a thousand years.
The district hereabouts has a sad story of its own. A
short time ago a man rose up and gathered the
fellahs to his standard, which was that of a new
religion. His following increased rapidly, and he
refused to disband at the summons of the Viceroy's
officers. A body of regular troops was sent against
them, and not far from Benisoueff the advance
guard, with six guns, came on the rebel or fanatic
leader. Ignorant of the nature of cannon, he at
once led his band to the attack. The guns opened
on them with grape, and mowed down lanes in the
multitude. Among the slain, killed by the first discharge, lay the leader of the men, whom he had
comforted with the assurance that he was invulner-
able. So far Ali Bey told us; but he did not add
what Lady Duff Gordon asserts, that there was a
wholesale desolating war of extermination—if war
it could be called—carried on against the wretches
who fled, and that thousands were hunted down
and put to death.

We went so slowly that the fear grew on us lest
Cook's tourists should overhaul the flotilla. But at
3 o'clock we arrived off Benisoueff, a large town
with a population varying from 45,000 (according
to a cavass translated by Hamed) to 15,000,

according to another native authority, and to
5,000, according to Ali Bey and Colonel Stanton.
There was a line of troops on the bank to act
as a guard of honour. A great number of
sheiks in white turbans were in attendance, and
a crowd of 400 or 500 people, men and boys,
turned out to sit on the bank, which was as
good a place to sit on as anywhere else. There
was a Palace of the Viceroy at our disposal, if
needed. Where has the Viceroy not got a Palace?
And where is there not a Palace of the Viceroy?
There was a pleasant Governor or Deputy-Governor
in waiting, and a great heap of cavasses with
scimitars and belts full of pistols. Hamed—excellent Hippopotamus Johnny, ever willing, always
showing his white teeth in a smile when he
is asked a question or desired to make himself
useful—led a detachment up the plank on shore,
and took his way along the bank of the river
towards the town. He was joined by a cavass,
who was a thing of terror to the small boys and
other backsheesh hunters. Capital fellow, indeed,
is Hamed, but a bad fellow to go astern of in fine
sand with the wind strong ahead. His red shoes
are lovely to look at, but they are spiked at the top
as if meant to shovel up the dust; and, if that be

the object, the designer must be congratulated on
rare success. The dust *was* blinding. Our way
lay through a ragged parade-ground extending
from the Pasha's house near the landing - place
to the mud-walled enclosure around the garden
of the Governor, inside which were visible the
jalousied windows of a neat residence. The town
looked like a village surrounded by a wall. We
entered the main street, which was about twelve feet
wide, and wound right and left through lines of

buildings, two storeys in height, of which the outer
wall facing the street was often only a brown bank
of mud, pierced by an opening for the closed portals.
On and on, meeting no one save frightened children
or timid women, who bolted into doorways like
rabbits in a warren at the approach of the fowler.
Such a chattering of voices as they made when

safe inside! From the suburb we turned into
the Bazaar. I strongly advise any one who may
read these notes not to halt at Benisoueff without doing the same. The street rambles at will,
bordered by shops, to which the arts of the
Frank are unknown. It is covered in at the
top, and the rays of light fall through the chinks
of the matting and boards in pillar-like shafts,
producing wonderful effects of light and shade.
The sellers were more interesting than their wares,
not but what there were strange things in confectionery and utensils and clothing of various
kinds, to be seen mixed up with Austrian cut-
lery and Manchester cottons. The owners scarcely
moved their eyes as the strangers passed. Young
and old, all apathetic, indifferent to commercial
enterprise, thinking it ungentlemanly, perchance, to
solicit custom. There were no crowds such as may
be seen at Cairo or Stamboul, but each shop had
a wee clientelle of its own, who, if they bought
nothing, kept the keeper in conversation. There
were barbers in active employ; scribes writing letters
which have to undergo the various vicissitudes
to which the "Poste Regie Egiziane" will expose
them; tin-plate workers, where Egyptians of six
or seven years of age were assiduously tinkering

and soldering pots and pans; butchers, fly infested;
kibob makers, whose shops sent forth the odour
of savoury meats; khans and cafés, and the omni-
present tobacco merchant, the various traders keeping well together, as if to promote wholesome com-
petition, or distract the intending buyer. In and
out, right and left, the street wound in its shady
course, the cavass shoving or thumping a way for us
through the crowd till once more we threaded a lane,
silent save when a dog uttered its yelp of alarm,
or the bully turkey-cock, sunning himself on a flat
roof, gobbled defiance to the noisy intruding infidels.
Now we passed a sombre mosque, and could see
the scattered worshippers, and hear the hum of
their low prayer. Stopping to investigate the cause
of a tremendous Babel, we discovered a school
of little ones packed as close as could be in a
dark cave-like room, who were following the master
in chorus as he read out a lesson from a large
slate. The master, a young man of twenty or
twenty-five years of age, seated on his hams, once
turned to look at us, and then, as though to set
his flock a good example, like him in the " Ancient
Mariner," "turned no more his head." Beside him,
in the place of honour, was a swell scholar, a big-
wig's son, splendid in embroidered jacket; but the

most of the forty or fifty boys and girls belonged, one might guess, to the lower stratum of the middle classes, — bright-eyed, white-teethed, they stared at us with all their might, and gave glances of great meaning to where the cavass, sword and all, darkened the entrance, whilst they kept shouting out their lessons.　And there were bad boys among them, I am sorry to say—Egyptian Jack Horners who had no pie to eat, but sat right doleful in corners, with faces turned to the wall, gazing at large sums set forth on cruel slates.　An infant truant who toddled in with a make-believe face that "it was all right," was pounced on by a boy-usher, armed with a rod, and at once provided with a calculation which it would puzzle the eminent Bidder to solve.

Having exhausted the sights of Benisoueff we returned to the steamer, which was making up supplies of coal.　Strings of children were carrying loads in baskets on their heads, whilst the men looked on, or now and then quickened them up with a stick.　A gang of girls arrived with cakes for the crew, but they were not allowed or would not come on board.　At the shore end of the gangway they put down their baskets, and the master of the flock and some boys carried the

cakes to the steamer. There was a striking proof
of the force of example. An infant Egyptian,
quite naked, was condemning himself to voluntary
slavery on the bank under our eyes. He could
not have been more than three years old, but he
was assiduously piling lumps of coal on a cab-
bage-leaf on the top of his head, and resolutely
picking them up when they fell from his little pate,
as though he meant to earn his pay, and not shirk
his self-appointed task. It was a glorious sunset.
The wind fell, and with it the dusk, but the sun
dipped into a warm bath of crimson, and threw
up splashes of orange and gold into the sky ere he
sank. It was dark before the Prince came up and
moored close to us. The Consul's dragoman caught,
on a night-line, a huge siluroid, which Professor
Owen carried off to the Prince with the hook in
its mouth. There was the usual stroll on the
bank before dinner, and in the evening most of the
party on board the Duke's steamer were invited
to join the Royal circle.

February 8th.—Cold night, windy morning, clouds
of dust, all windows and ports closed. There was
less trouble concerning the tubbing arrangements,
as a screen has been fitted up on deck which
permits the natives on shore to view the eccentric

M

proceedings of the stranger, but hides him from the crew. Grievous things have occurred. The net which was intended to ensnare the solitary crocodile turned out yesterday to be adapted rather for the capture of the multitudinous herring. It is too much to expect that the crocodile will prove obliging, and, out of pure civility, believe he is a herring. Then, again, the night-line, from which a good deal was expected, came to nought. The hook was baited with the entrails of a fowl, which proved very tempting to some monster of the deep. But he was strong and tyrannous : in a contest of "pull monster, pull dragoman," the line broke, and we saw not the conqueror.

Benisoueff was probably wide awake when the flotilla cast off from the banks at dawn, but the world on board, save Reis, captain, and crew, was fast asleep. The Duke's steamer led. For the first time in ten years, it is said, a shower of rain fell this morning; and why it fell it is hard to conceive, inasmuch as a wind strong enough to blow it into mist rushed down the stream, and raised clouds of sand along the shore, which rendered it impossible to see the banks at times. A learned man prognosticated a fine day from the sunset last night. Alas, how wrong he was!

When the pattering of the rain ceased, the dust
rose. No effort could keep that fine torment from
going where it listed, and it liked to settle in
the cabins, and on beards, and up nostrils, and in
eyes. Of course this is an exceptional day; but
we are in for abnormal weather it seems.

The wind, cold enough as long as the boats were
under the bank, was exceedingly fierce when we
got out into the stream. Hour by hour it waxed in
power, cresting the dun-coloured waves with white
foam, till the sun was shrouded in clouds. These
grew denser, and produced the effect of a fog. The
palm-trees, moved into life by the blast, with stems
hidden by the lower and heavier strata of the volatile
sand-banks, threw their feathery leaves like " knightly
plumes " in their play. A yellowish screen shut out
the Nile, yielding occasionally, so as to show
through the rifts the low-lying shores—here covered
with sugar-cane in patches, there bare and desert-
like—lined with high banks, or barred by mounds
of limestone.

Pumping-machines for irrigation, and tall chimneys, denoted the existence of the rich sugar districts
which we heard of but could not see.

The fellah men and women, with garments
streaming in the blast, seemed as much annoyed

by the unusual storm as we were. A valetudinarian sent from England by a doctor, and encountering such an afternoon, would, if he were an irritable and unjust-minded person, not disposed to be charitable in respect to climatic irregularities, wish that his medical adviser were out in his place. We thought of the Suez Canal when we saw the dun and yellow clouds, which seemed able to fill up whole seas.

As the Prince's boat was not visible when we got as far as Feshn, a village with two mosques, our boat was put in to shore and secured. Sumner took his gun, carried off "Hippopotamus Johnny," and, accompanied by Colonel Marshall and myself, walked across the fields towards a small village shrouded in palm-trees, and distinguished by a mosque and minaret, and a tomb-like structure ; but there was nothing to be met with except natives, domestic pigeons, hawks, and larks. A pigeon fell first, but as if in revenge at his undeserved and illegitimate fate, dropped into a patch of long grass, in which two amateur beaters sought in vain to discover it ; a buzzard was also unlucky, and finally some sort of wild beast—fox, jackal, or wolf—*les trois se disent*—was rolled over, but got up again and escaped in the growing crops. Outside the village is a railway station, and at it were waiting one turkey-cock, two hens, ten dogs, and two natives. As the Royal flotilla was coming up, the party abandoned any attempt to improve their minds by investigating the village, and got on board. Then we all set off together, and, for ever pelted by wind and sand, got into a wider Nile which opened out at times like a lake.

Arrived at Aboo Girgeh at 4 P.M., passing Shekh Embarak, a lofty mountain ridge which comes close down to the water's edge. The Royal steamer did not come up for nearly an hour later. The Prince went off in the punt with Webster, and made a good shot, getting seven spoonbills and two black storks; then netted the river, and had two hauls, one a blank, the other bringing in some small fish, which were cooked for dinner. There were plenty of wild geese, but they were very much alive to danger, and kept circling high in air, uttering a prolonged trumpet-like cry to warn their brethren.

Towards sundown the steamers sidled in to the left bank at Sheik Fodl, 122 miles from Cairo, to make fast for the night.

It would be slow work if all the places mentioned by Murray were to be inspected, for the Nile becomes a water way, with landing-places for the antiquary at every mile. The limestone ridges which hedge the Desert here sweep down close to the right bank, and tower above the traveller.

February 9th.—The thermometer 58°. Soon after our departure from the mooring stakes at Sheik Fodl, what should come on but a dense fog! It is very seldom indeed such an unpleasant hindrance to navigation occurs on the Nile; but it so happened that as we had wind and rain yesterday, there was a fog this morning; not one of your dense choking yellow mediums, in which the lungs contend with an enemy of potency, but a soft white milky cloud, more like a rainless Scotch mist (if such a thing there can be) than anything else. So there was a great sounding of steam whistles, and the steamers lay to on the river, just giving a turn now and then to keep their bows to the stream.

We saw nothing of the ruins, of which Sheik Fodl boasted two, till modern science improved them away into materials for the sugar manufactory at Minieh. Nor did we visit the pits in which the fathers of village dogs, in all the comfort of embalmment, are buried with the mummies of their owners or well-wishers, each of whom, like the untutored Indian, seemed to think that,—

> Admitted to the equal sky,
> His faithful dog should bear him company.

Nor did we see "Mary's Well" (Bir Sitti
Mariam), a cave in a rock, wherein the Nile water
rises during the flood, near which the Copts still
bury their dead. In an hour, as soon as the fog
cleared off, the steamers headed up stream as hard
as they could, passing the limestone quarries of
Sheik Hassan, and its remains, Golosanch, and the
quarries of E' Serareeh, in which Sir Gardner Wilkinson states two painted grottoes existed, belonging
to the early reign of Pthahmen, son of Rameses
the Great. One was destroyed by the Turks; the
other still remains, thanks to Sir Gardner's exertions with the Viceroy.

We were coming up to the famous Gebel-e-Tayr
—very like Gibraltar that name—the mountain, or
rather lofty ridge, where the birds of Egypt meet
annually in Parliament assembled, and select a
victim who is to stay on the rock for a year.
He may not be a victim, indeed—he may be an
honoured bird; whether he is called on to "sing"
all the time I cannot say, but, any way, the bird
being placed en faction, is deserted by the whole
Parliament, which flies off to Greece, whence it
returns in a year to liberate the sentinel, and to
choose another to take his place. From an odd
fortress-looking building, with low cupolas and

mud buttresses, placed on the plateau of this ridge, divers natives were rushing violently down the steep, and diving headlong into the stream; they swam out towards the flotilla, dropping down on them in the current reckless of paddle-wheels, with black heads bobbing up and down in the water like fishermen's buoys.

" Look at those naked black fellows! Look at them jumping into the river! Pirates? Oh, Reis! Robbers, or madmen? What do they want?" There is a scarce concealed smile of contempt on the Mahometan's face. "No, only Christians, effendi!"

And soon they are alongside, clutching at the rudder, and striving to grasp the sides of the dahabeahs, whilst they shout out, sputtering, "Baksheesh, O Hawadjee! Ana Christianne ya Hawadjee!" These are the brethren of the Coptic convent, Sitteh Mariam el Adrah (Our Lady Mary the Virgin), which is also called Dehra el Bukkar, or "Convent of the Pulley," from the means employed to raise food, and to gather in the holy fathers. They got nothing but a good swim for their pains. I think that they would give a mile in two to any Christian brotherhood in the world, and beat them in a fair swimming-match; but our native friends did not think much of them, or of Copts in

general, and spoke of these as intolerant Christians
speak of Jews in more civilized lands.   The old
Church of Africa seems dead in faith and in works.
It has added another instance to the many which
refute the dogma that persecution is a fostering
power to the truth.

From what I hear, there seems but little likelihood that the ancient light will be reillumined for
many a year to come in this once Christian land.
It is the land in which, thousands of years ago,
the Lord worked miracles, and the hearts of the
people are hardened now, as was that of Pharaoh.
To all preachings and warnings they have been
obdurate.   Saints have taught and suffered, and
fathers of the Church have evangelized, and there
is the Egyptian now, whatever may be said of
his future, as devout an infidel as when he was
the follower of strange gods, against whom Moses
lifted up his voice and his rod.   The march of
civilization passes over his body, and leaves its
impress on the outer man.   Rulers, enlightened and
energetic, drive their car over the quivering mass.
All in vain.   There does not exist the influence
which led nations to change their faith at the
bidding of a king. The Egyptians are not to be
converted, as the Britons were, by the example of a

ruler, who, indeed, would be rash if he tried to Christianize himself.

The Copts are now reckoned at no more than 100,000 souls. Many have gone over to the Church of Rome, and so rapid were the conversions that the Government took measures to check the influences to which they were said to be due. So, in Egypt at least, human power can mar the agencies which are said to be too powerful for State interference in countries nearer home, inasmuch as the conversions were very rapidly put a stop to. It is certain that in some quarters here, Roman Catholicism is looked on as a peculiar French power, and is dreaded, or rather discouraged, on that account.

At Meghara the flotilla lay to, in order that the Prince might get a shot at the numerous flocks of birds on the banks. They are very wary at this time of year, but the Prince is patient and never loses a chance. On this occasion he managed to get twenty-eight flamingoes at one shot.

The river here becomes tortuous, with lofty limestone rocks on the right bank, cut into fantastic shapes; on the left, sand-banks and rich alluvial fields, lined with date palms. It is a peculiarity

of our navigation that no one can tell where we
will pull up at night. Certainly the inquiring
stranger will get no assistance from the native
sailors, Reis, or captain. If you ask, "When
shall we arrive?"—the answer is, "God grant
you facilities." Ask "How far it is"—the
answer is, "As God pleases." "Do you think
we shall reach Nileville to-night?"—"It depends
on God." Ali Bey was so contraried by the
difficulty of getting at time or distances in his
journeyings up the river, that he constructed an
itinerary for himself, and I am bound to add that
his mileage differs very materially from that of
Mr. Murray.

Small bodies of horsemen were in attendance
at various points along the banks, to give assistance and direct the course of the steamers through
the sand-banks. The Ornament of the Two Seas
steamed ahead of the Royal steamers, which waited
for the Prince's punt, and at 2.30 P.M. arrived at
Minieh. A Governor, or Bey, and his suite were
in attendance, a gathering of the curious cavasses
and sheiks grouped on the banks of the river.
Two standards floated from flag-staffs at the head
of a flight of wooden steps at the landing-place.
Long before we reached the city — if it may be

called so — the tall chimney — not quite safe or straight, by the bye — of the Viceroy's sugar factory was in view before us, tainting the air with a column of smoke; and when we landed and got through introductions and salutations, we were led to the factory, which fronts the river.

There is a large plant of machinery by Derosne, Cail, & Co., of Paris; but the cane is put between the rollers by men, instead of being gathered in by the machine. The furnaces under the boilers are fed by the refuse of the cane, which is carried away and spread out to dry in the sun, after it has been crushed. The heat and glare, the swarthy figures, nearly naked, toiling, with strange cries and yells, at the never-ending work of feeding the many gaping furnace-mouths with the light fuel, which blazed away in a series of flash-like outbursts, suggested an Inferno. We had to mount the top of the boiler to inspect the crushing machinery, and then take a look at the refining pans and operations. The number of young girls and boys moving about in the smothering atmosphere did not produce an agreeable effect, and we were glad to be released from statistical researches and get into the air.

Out of doors there was one of those spectacles too common in Egypt. A procession of girls, from

five to twelve years of age, was moving up an
inclined plane to the second story of a building
where the masons were at work, each with a heavy
basket of bricks, or heap of mortar on her head.
Poor little creatures! They sang a wailing sort of
song, all together, as if to give them heart for
their work.

Another procession descended at the same time.
It seemed as if their song was lighter and more
cheerful. They had got rid of the load, and if
they were going for another, at least they had not
reached it yet. Some, seated in a circle on the
ground, were eating from a pile of coarse, brown,
ill-baked cakes of maize flour; others were mixing
mortar with their hands. Boys and girls, half-
naked, were sweeping up the fragments of cane
which fell from the loaded camels that came in
solemn file ceaselessly from the fields with their rich
burthens. These were thrown on the ground of the
outer yard, and formed in large heaps, whence they
were removed in armfuls by the men, who took them
to the crushing mills. The factory can turn out 500
kantars of 100lb. each in the day, and has produced
60,000 kantars in the year. The sugar, which fetches
about 4½d. a pound, is very white and exceedingly
sweet. The refuse molasses is sold to the natives,

in large sealed jars, and there is also a rum or raki
factory in connection with the factory. The establishment is one of the more important enterprises
of the Viceroy, and is worked on his account with
very profitable results. He employs 1,500 camels for
transport, not to speak of steamers, barges, &c. The
men get 6*d*., the children 3*d*., a day for their work,
which is not bad considering the price of provisions.
The Prince and Princess arrived in the evening, but
it was too dark for them to visit the factory.

There was nothing to be seen in the town. The
Governor has a pretty garden, and there is a fair
market; the bazaar was shut. As we strolled along
the bank of the river after dinner—a very hazardous
process by the bye, if it were not for the animated
lamp-posts who line it—we came on a boy sitting
in the darkness gravely under a tree, with a tray
full of tomatoes. It was odd to find a young tomato
merchant so full of faith in customers as to stay
out at night in hope of a person coming to buy.
But on inquiry, the affair wore a different aspect.
Ali Bey averred that the boy had been put there to
watch the basket by a man who had stolen the
tomatoes from the Governor's garden. He, seeing
Ali Bey, fled to the outer darkness of sugar-cane,
and intended to couch there till we left, in which

case he would come back for his tomatoes or his money.

On our arrival some one wanted to send a telegram to Cairo to ask after our mails; but the office was closed. It is the custom of the country to become stone dead from 12 till 3 o'clock. There was the English telegraphist, Mr. George—a very good artist, by the way—on board the Consul-General's steamer, and he was set to work to wake up the clerks along the line; but, though specially warned, and, as might be supposed, expectant of the Royal progress, these gentlemen had cleverly cut off all communication with Cairo, and for hours the needle made no sign. Very probably the clerks will hear something not at all to their advantage for the artful stratagem. We are very apt to regard the ways of those who have not our ways just as the Greeks looked on the fashions of those whom they styled Barbarians. The Egyptians, who rise with the sun, would regard our shopkeepers and clerks as lazy ne'er-do-wells for lying in bed till 7 or 8 o'clock on a summer morning. It will be some time ere they are vexed with the habits and customs of people connected with the daily press.

CHAPTER VII.

BENI HASSAN.—ALI RISA.—EGYPTIAN POOR LAWS.—
FISHING AND SHOOTING.—WATER-CARRIERS.—SIOOT.
—THE JEREED.

Wednesday, February 10th.—(Minich.) A lovely
sunrise. As the dawn grew into day long flights
of geese streaked the horizon—spoonbills, cranes,
and flamingoes were visible stalking about on
the margin of the sand-bank just opposite our
boats. It was remarkable how silent they were.
They were too hungry, perhaps, to cry out, or
too wary to call attention to their doings at an
early hour, when they were relying on our sleepiness,
and venturing almost within shot. The Prince, to
try their craft, his own and Webster's, resolved to
remain at Minich, "two shots at least" from the big
gun having been promised to him. The Zenet el
Bahareen did not go off till 8 A.M., leaving the
Royal party behind. We were anxious to visit the
monuments at Beni Hassan above, though we could

not read their records of old-world history. Our
course lay up a broader and more expanded Nile,
the landscape only varied by the shape of the limestone formations on the right bank, by patches of
palms, dates, and cultivated land, and by the
changing outline of the distant horizon of the
Desert. The day was warm, the sun bright, vast
quantities of geese, pelicans, ducks, cormorants,
herons, and cranes on the sand-banks—no crocodile.
It is a wonder there is even a bird, for the
shouting of pilots on land and in boats rings on
all sides.

About two hours and a half paddling upwards
brought us to the right bank below the caves of Beni
Hassan. Before the steamer arrived at the mooring-
place a polk of irregular cavalry came in view,
capering along the sand. They were sheiks, who
had been warned to wait with their horses for
our party; and as the vessel came to the shore
the horsemen, dismounting, stood by their steeds
to welcome us, and the children of Hassan, young
and old, formed on the top in groups to inspect
the arrival. Between the slope of sand, covered
with boulders, which extends from the base of the
cliff, there is a patch of cultivated land overflowed
by the Nile at its rise, on which there is a small

N

village; southwards there are the remains of two
larger villages—almost towns—which have a story.
It is short.   Ibrahim Pasha made an example of the
inhabitants.   They were as a race rather given to
predatory practices, stopping boats, levying black-
mail, and picking and stealing generally.   So the
ruler of the land made a swoop on them: such as
he could catch at the first flight he slew, the others
were sent to live in scattered villages; and, to make
the place a sort of awful warning, he forbade any one
to reside in the two towns.   Not a soul lives, nor is
any one allowed to harbour, in the roofless houses,
the walls of which stand erect and apparently quite
fit for use.   The excavated tombs, of which "Murray"
gives a good account, lie inland about a mile from
the present shore.   They are confined to one level or
stratum of the rock, and extend for about three-
quarters of a mile.   A short ride over the fields, few
of which were under crop, brought us to the sandy
ascent to the ridge on which are the grottoes and
mummy depositories.

Dismounting, we climbed in single file up to a
ledge, which forms a kind of esplanade in front
of the line of grottoes.   Although the weight of
evidence and of learned opinion is against the
impression, it is scarcely possible to believe, at

first sight, that these excavations, or cut-out chambers, were not intended for human residences.
The ceilings are vaulted; externally, there are
few ornaments. The roof of each chamber is
supported on pillars, which divide it into three
parts. These pillars differ in character; some are
polygons, with abacus; others represent, it is
supposed, water reeds, with capitals of lotus:
some are of the natural colour of the stone;
others are stained red. The walls are covered with
hieroglyphs, and in most of the chambers are deep
mummy pits cut down in the rock, with the
indents still visible by which the mummies were
lowered to their resting-places. On the sides of
the chambers, there is displayed for us, as in a
panorama, the whole life of the people who made
them. We see them engaged in war and in
hunting, in manufactures and in commerce, in
fishing, in playing. We see the trophies of their
victories—a procession of prisoners from Asia, says
Sir Gardner Wilkinson, because the men have
beards and the women ankle-boots—nay, we know
—our wise men say so—the name of their chief,
Absha; and of his people, Mes-segur; and of
the owner of the tomb, Nefoth; and the date of
his being, viz. in the reign of Osirtasen I. and II.,

N 2

who reigned long ere Joseph came into Egypt.
Barbers are shaving and nail-cutting; glass-blowers
are at work; statuaries; wrestlers contending, red
and black, in pairs; criminals undergoing punish-
ment; members of chess-clubs engaged at their
game; the birds and animals of forest and plain,
and the fishes of sea and river. M. Victor Hugo
would be horrified to hear that the comprachicos
practised their trade in the time of the Pharaohs;
for the critics aver that certain curious people,
depicted on the walls, are dwarfs and deformed
persons in the suite of grandees! It has been
remarked that the horse does not appear in the
more ancient Egyptian monuments, and that the
first representations of it are found in those of
the eighteenth dynasty, about 1,500 years B.C.

We wandered from chamber to chamber in
wonder, not always silent, Professor Owen examining stones; Mr. Fowler measuring; each man
interpreting, after his fashion, the scenes painted
in blue, red, and black on the walls. In our train
came all the Italian servants and the Turkish
chibouquejees—for note that these latter are like
our shadows; sometimes they precede instead of
following, and go on shore whenever we do;
generally, too, selecting, as we discovered, the

best horses, and delighting to scour the plain, with our pipe-stems, like bundles of fishing-rods, under their arms. It was worth while to notice the interest taken in the grottoes by the Europeans, and the utter indifference manifested by the Turks. The cares of the former were divided between providing us with slight animal comforts, lugged up from the steamer, and seeing the caves. The latter were intent on making coffee and preparing our pipes, exclusively.

Interesting as the excavations are, there is a grievance and an eyesore intolerable in every cave. The army of Snobland has been upon them. It is some consolation that few English names could be made out, though one "C. B. Elliott," in 1868, cut his name boldly on the rock of a temple, and Brown, Jones, and Robinson have left their marks.

There was a great terror on the fellah sheiks and their followers who were with us—a silence so unusual to those who know what it is to be persecuted for baksheesh, that it invited inquiry. Well, Ali Risa, later in the day, as we were all sitting on the ledge of rocks, enjoying the beautiful view of the Nile valley as it spread its sheet of green, like a broad riband laid down in the midst of the Desert

sand-hills, admitted that he had something to do
with it. But what that something was he would not
tell : it was a matter which had happened to himself
years ago, when he visited the place in company with
M. de Lesseps' family, and the result of which was
that the sheik then and there present would like very
much a chance of putting a bullet into Ali Bey's
interior ; whence it may be surmised that the said
sheik was rather the worse in some way for the
transaction.

Whenever Ali Risa went away for a moment there
was a fellah man or boy by one's side, pointing to
the palm of his hand, and uttering softly that horrid
dissyllable—" Baksheesh." Little boys then bore
down boldly with calcareous casts of marine shells
and held them aloft, with the words, " Antic ! Antic !
Baksheesh !" till the redoubtable Bey's fez came in
view, when they collapsed at once. Returning a little
in advance of the party towards the steamer, I had a
proof of either the blindness or the cunning of the
fellah. I rode towards the village, and came between
it and a little girl, who was tending goats in
some high grass on the sand-hill. The instant she
saw me, the frightened creature abandoned her
charge, and with piercing cries fled towards her
home. Her wailing increased in shrillness as she

perceived I cut off her retreat. She darted past the horse as I reined up, and, sobbing still, ran into a hovel in front of me. A piece of silver could not tempt her near, and so I threw it on the sand, and pointed out the spot to the probable father and mother, who came out of the house. It was under their noses, but they could not see it. They were joined by others in the search, and all squatting down within a yard of where it lay bright and shining in the sun, either looked or made believe to look for it, poking about with their fingers, till one old fellow scraped the sand over it; and so I left them groping assiduously, and hope they got it. On arriving at the steamer, there was a little excitement going on in connection with an old fisherman, who with the aid of a couple of men was spreading a hand-net in the river: one end of it was fastened to an earthen jar, another to a buoy, and when they had payed the net out from the boat it floated upright down stream. The boat, hailed by Hamed, came alongside, and the old fellow handed up a basket of fish, which was brought to Professor Owen. He identified five species among the twelve fish—three siluroids, the bagrus and apirtes—a fish like a carp, which Hamed says attains the weight of 120 lb. in the Upper Nile—and others.

Then we had nothing to do. Even luncheon was eaten—a light one, *only* caviare and tunny fish, sardines, tongue, ham, rice, various jams, fruit, Sauterne, claret, soda-water, coffee, and pipes. Dolce far niente came on us as on the natives, who sat chattering on the banks. This is their easy time, poor fellows! Soon they will be toiling with heads in the sun, and legs in the water, for weary days and weeks and months. It is pleasant to sit under the awning on deck, and gaze on the water flashing in the hot sun—to peer into dreamland—to wander away there till we are lost, self, identity, and all! Hark! There is a trumpet-sound from the very heart of dreamland, summoning the airy hosts of its armies to battle! It is only an easy snore from the cabin. But it wakes us up. It is not to be endured thus to dawdle away our time. What is to be seen through the glass? Nothing save sails and the smoke of two sugar-factory chimneys—most odious signs of civilization in the land of the Pharaohs. Stay! There is a magnificent eagle placidly floating down the river on a carcase. He is far away; Mr. Fowler takes a rifle and tries to stalk the bird-king, but as he creeps among the sand-hills, two jackals dash out of the fields far below, and the eagle, rising slowly from his ignoble prey, alights on a sand-bank. Fowler

got a shot at a jackal, but it was a long one, and
the rifle threw high.   I tried my fortune with the
eagle as he sat on the opposite bank, and sighting
Whitworth for 300 yards, sent a bullet so straight
that the on-lookers thought it broke his leg.   The
sand flew up over him ; but the eagle rose from the
midst of his courtier crows and ravens, and circled
away to some securer roosting-place.   It was now
4 o'clock, and there was no sight of our Prince or
his fleet.   We open our mail-bags which were de-
livered last night.

Is it ill-natured to confess that we read of skating
in London and Paris, and of snow storms, with
some sort of selfish delight in our hot sun and
warm wind?   To-day was heavenly—a day in
which to live was enough for all the outer sense,
and in which the inner life was possessed by a calm
serenity.

In the *Times* there was a heart-rending account of
" Death by Starvation"—a woman and her infant
starved to death in Christian millionaire London—
si plein d'or et de misère.   Her husband driven mad !

What a reproach to us, to hear Ali Risa, apropos
of the way in which slaves run away to the Soudan,
explain how, by the law of the land, every sheik is
obliged to feed all comers for the night, and give

them lodging, so that no man can starve in this poor benighted heathen land. Slaves can or could thus escape to their pet Soudan. Whilst we were waiting for the Prince, a mild excitement was created by throwing small coin on shore, which led to furious and protracted controversy among sheiks, men and boys, in which an idiot took a large part, and, as is often the way of the world, got the money. Towards dusk the Royal steamers appeared. When the fleet was moored, the Prince started for a large sand-bank opposite, and we had two draws of the net, and caught one small fish, which was not a rich reward for the labour of twenty-five or thirty people—hard labour in tugging at ropes and shouting vigorously—hard for the men, who had to carry us to and from the boats over soft mud, and land the fishermen on the bank, and row them back. The Prince takes great delight in this, or would do so if the net would draw anything in the shape of fish to shore. The failure of the net is a misfortune. I believe it was left to a distinguished naval officer to see that the net was all right. Why to a naval officer? Nets are used in fresh water, nets are used in salt water; but what an admiral can know about the sort of article which is best suited to catch fish in the Nile more or better than any other man, I am at a loss to

guess or imagine, unless it be that the said admiral
is very fond of fishing with nets. The result may be
described in a few words: there are no fish caught.
The net is rowed carefully out to a shelving sand-
bank; one end is landed and given over to a party of
amateurs invited from the flotilla generally and to
the four sailors of the Ariadne, who "work" the
fishing and the boating, and keep the shoulders of
the Egyptian mariners to the wheel. One squad is
landed to man the shore end of the rope, and the
boat is then rowed off, making a wide sweep, and
returning to shore with the other end, which is seized
by party No. 2. Then with a pull all together the
ropes are dragged in, the Prince working as hard as
the best of them,—the sailors in the water, the
amateurs shouting and slipping in the soft sand;
nearer and nearer comes what ought to be the purse.
It is landed at last. It is empty. Not a fin. "Oh,
deuce take Admiral Blank!"

The Duke and his friends were invited to
dine on board the Royal steamer; and Achmet
Hassan, the Captain, was asked to join the
party, whom he entertained by his liveliness
and good-humour, and by the expressiveness of
his broken English, in which he managed to make
hard hits. He remembered, when on a visit to

England years ago, seeing the Prince—"nice small
boy," and before dinner was over he rose amid
cheering and laughter, and proposed the "Health
of the Queen of England," and added, "Get you
all up, you know." The Prince of Wales then gave
the "Health of His Highness the Viceroy," which
was warmly received. The Governor of Sioot, Abdé
Bey, who came down to meet the Prince and Princess after dinner, was also invited, and had pipes
and coffee on board.

Thursday, February 11th.—To make up for our
delay, which, if not dull, was becoming fraught
with danger of being overtaken by the Tourists,
the little fleet started at 4 o'clock this morning
from Beni Hassan. There was a sensible shock
given to our vessel soon after we left, which awoke
most of the sleepers. A mass of earth detached
itself from a bank of the river and fell into the
water, creating a wave which splashed violently
against the side, and threw the water into the
windows of some of the cabins. There must be
frequent changes produced by such agencies in the
riverine farms, as in the Mississippi lands, where a
man may find a good slice of his estate gone when
he wakes in the morning.

It must not be imagined that the Royal pro-

gress makes a great sensation in the country side.
The servants of the Governor, the local officers,
and the cavasses, are surrounded by a crowd of the
curious — water-carriers, and idlers; but the im-

mense mass of
the populace
is untouched.
The women
are rarely to
be seen in the
crowd. A knot
of them here
and there,
coming down
to fill their
water-jars at the landing-places, linger a moment
or two longer perhaps than usual, and peep out
above the folds of their dresses at the steamers;

but it is a languid interest after all, and they
stalk back, camel-like, swaying easily under their
heavy burthens, to their homes, and cast no
lingering look behind. They do not care how far
they expose their legs—at least, they go as far as
any Highlander, and not quite so far as a ballet-
girl; but they are most careful as to neck and
shoulders; and I don't think of the hundreds we
have seen one has permitted the eye to rest on so
much of the upper section of the torso as is so
kindly authorized by fashion to be a correct com-
promise with the nude. It may be inferred that
there is no very definite idea in their minds as to
who the Prince of Wales is, and that they do not
know much beyond the limits of their own village
and the local potentate.

The whole of the day was a marvel of loveliness,
to be marked with the whitest of chalk. The Nile
passes—more properly speaking, rushes—through a
richer country. There are sugar plantations, which
need manufactories at Rhoda, and elsewhere, to con-
sume the produce. There are more verdant fields
and broader patches of cultivation. The waterworks
are more frequent, and the labours of the shadoof
more constant. The stream is covered with sails,
or boats impelled against the wind by rowers tug-

ging at great oars, to the rhythm of a plaintive
chorus. Then we come to a high range of rock
on the right bank, Gibel Aboofayda, and catch
glimpses of the Desert encroaching here and there.
There were heaps of birds along the shore; prodigious multitudes of blue and grey herons on the
rocks spoke of plenty of fish in the river. Passing
the rocks of Aboofayda, the Prince made some
excellent shots at individual cormorants, swarms of
which were roosting and flying about the recesses
of these grand cliffs. The range of limestone on
our left is bored in all directions by square aper-
tures, leading to the chambers, in which mummies
of sacred animals and possibly those of men were
buried. The navigation became very difficult, and
even our light steamer went once aground.
The river winds and twists like a snake, and
is as mischievous. A large town which we
passed towards evening, Manfaloot, was half destroyed some years ago by the washing away of
the bank on which it stood. Here we shot by
two dahabeahs, one with the British, another with
the United States flag; and farther on we overtook a very large and handsome boat flying the
French tricolour, which greeted the Prince subse-
quently, with a royal salute from pistols, double

barrel and single barrel, very enthusiastically.
Thanks to our gallant allies!

We saw Sioot for more than an hour-and-a-half,
ere our steamer could reach the landing-place at
dusk. There were considerable preparations to receive the Royal party. About thirty irregular
cavalry were drawn up on the bank, and the Governor,
Abdé Bey, and his functionaries, with horses, carriages, and any number of donkeys, were in waiting.
The shore was brilliantly illuminated. Sioot has a
population of 30,000 souls, and is a place of
great importance in Upper Egypt. It is the start-
ing-point and terminus of the caravans between
Dongola and the province. Our party disem-
barked and went through the town. A bright-eyed
boy, who joined in the informal procession of natives
in our train, burst out into very good English,

and shook hands with every one all round. He is
brother of the American Consul, who can speak
no English; and he learned to speak and write at
a school established by some American philanthro-
pists in the city. There is no British Consul;
but the Spaniards, of all people, have a functionary
of that description.

We visited in our ramble a school maintained by
the State, or, rather, passed in review a line of youths,
by no means remarkable for good looks, attired in
French cut frock-coats, red trousers with blue stripe,
and fez cap. They might have looked tolerable
in their native dress; but it would be difficult
to pick out a lot of more ill-favoured lads than
those fifty who were presented to us. There were
a number of others caught sight of at an open
door in a building in which they appeared to be
packed very close, but the door was shut on the
inquiring stranger as he approached. After visiting
the school, the party were entertained by the irregular cavalry, a few of whom went through the
exercise of the jereed. There was nothing very
remarkable about the showmen, except the wonderful
rapidity with which they reined up their horses,
checked and turned them at full speed. But the
leader, armed with a long lance, wielded it with

much expertness, and set a fine example to his troop,
who might be useful as light cavalry, and who certainly were very picturesque. It was long after
dark before the Prince's fleet came up at full
speed—rather a perilous feat in the night. The
Prince came on board the Duke's steamer after
dinner.

February 12th.—(Sioot.) A cold night; thermometer 58° at 9 A.M. It was a very disagreeable day
—a high wind and clouds of dust. The Duke's
party started after breakfast for Sioot, attended by
Hamed. The city lies about two miles from the
landing-place. The donkey boys were unusually
malignant and persecuting, and even Hamed had to
rouse himself to use strong language, which on some
occasions was rendered into muscular English by
the Chelebees. We set off, having asserted freedom
of election in the matter of donkeys, and made
a fine entrance into the city, which consists of the
usual mud-bricked houses, built anyhow, and caval-
caded the bazaar, made a solemn purchase of tar-
booshes and shot, at very fair prices, and returned
just as the Royal party was setting out for the
same visit. After breakfast the Prince and Princess,
attended by Mrs. Grey and suite, visited the city
and the American Mission School, under the charge

of the Rev. Mr. Hogg—eighty pupils. As it is
very likely many an Eton man who knows all
about the Po and the Tiber is ignorant of
the course of the Humber or the Tweed, so
the lads, who answered very creditably, were, to
Sir Samuel Baker's great astonishment, found
to be unacquainted with the sources of the
Nile. From the school the Royal travellers went
to the Mosque, and thence proceeded to the
Egyptian school, but the boys were absent, as it
was a Friday. The rooms, containing some twenty
beds, were well ventilated and comfortable. The
Princess, in mounting her horse, sustained what
Dr. Minter called a luxation of the thumb, which
gave her great pain for the time, and made tears
come to her eyes, but she never complained of it.
The Prince and Princess made purchases in the
bazaar, and went back to the fleet, which started
at 2.30 P.M. On returning to the vessels, natives
came on board with specimens of pottery, and
sold a number of jars, coloured very prettily red,
black, and white, of classical and elegant shapes.

The country around Sioot is very rich, and
spreads far along the banks of the river. The
course of the stream is tortuous, and the channel
difficult to keep. And here is a paradox: "If

the steamers get aground going up now, and the
river keeps falling every day till June, how on
earth are they to get back in March or April?"
Thus asks Inductive Inquiry. To whom replies
Experience in the shape of the Captain. And Ali
Bey replies: "The river goes down, indeed, but
as it does the shallows disappear, and the waters,
in a more contracted channel, scoop out better
marked channels." Voilà comme les choses s'ex-
pliquent! It is a NE. wind, which is a very
different sort of fellow from what he is in
England. On board the ship it is better than on
land, but still the dust blows into our cabins,
and it is too hot to shut the ports to keep it
out. Whether the river be less fishy here or not I
cannot say, but the absence of cormorants, compared
with their great abundance lower down, was remarkable; nor were flamingos, spoonbills, or ducks very
abundant. No crocodiles as yet. They are very
provoking. A reward is to be given for showing
one—usual fee 10 piastres—if he be slain, the
reward to the first demonstrator is 40 piastres. Be
sure the Arabs and fellahs are keen enough to look
out for them. But our great following, and the
noise of the paddles of so many steamers, not to
speak of the shouting of the men employed to keep

watch and ward over our course, have given the alarm
to the timid water-lizards, which, between the constant "potting" of dahabeah sportsmen, and the
never-ceasing persecutions to which infant members
of the family are exposed, lead a troublous life
below the First Cataract.

The Prince's stuffer, Mr. Baker, has a workshop
on deck in the bow, formed of canvas and marked
"private," but is not unfrequently aggressed upon
by collectors of feathers for fly-tying. Science is
always exposed to the interruptions of the outer
world. He has got in a forward state spoonbills,
flamingos, mallard, merlin, hawk-owl, herons, cranes,
cormorants, hoopoes, doves, but of land game birds
little or none. I doubt if ever any one visited
the Nile under more favourable circumstances, so
far as the means of enjoying it are concerned; but
the Prince is not acting in accordance with the
advice given to travellers of seeing everything
while he can, and not putting it off till he returns,
as every one hopes he will.

At an hour before sunset the fleet turned bows in-
shore, and the mooring stakes were driven into the
bank near a village called Isbah. The Prince and a
few friends went out shooting, and got some pigeons,
a small owl, a hoopoe, &c. They were attended by

a crowd, who were highly pleased when the Prince ordered money to be given for the pigeons he had killed. It is said that the natives do not like one to come after the pigeons close to the villages, as they are apt to fly away to other districts when persecuted by small shot, but that they do not care if the sportsmen go out into the fields. The villages swarm with pigeons, which are lodged far more comfortably than their owners, and the young ones are a very valuable addition to the limited resources of the poor fellah. There was a glorious sunset, the finest we have yet seen, over a distant line of Desert hills which closes the wide expanse of bearded wheat, dotted with dates and acacias, and here and there blurred by the brown heap which constitutes a fellah village, crouching under groves of palms.

CHAPTER VIII.

February 13th.—(Isbah.) One week to-day since
we left Cairo. The voyage seems to have proved
of service to the Princess, who looks better than
she did on arriving in Egypt. The fleet moved
off at 5.30 A.M., and went at a steady pace up the
river. A steamer was discerned following us far
off. "The tourists are coming!" was the universal cry. Every glass was directed to the ship. At
last she was pronounced to be a trading steamer
from Cairo, and a feeling of relief was at once ex-
perienced. At 9 o'clock, the immense cliffs of Gebel
Hareedi, towering perpendicularly upwards from the
sloping base of débris marked by the most enormous
boulders, presented a fine appearance. There was
some discussion as to their height. I estimated them
at 300 feet from the base of the débris. Mr. Fowler
put them at 700, which was surely too much. At
11 o'clock A.M. the steamers ran in and made fast to a

high bank, and after breakfast all hands went on
board the Royal steamer to hear Mr. Fowler read
his report on the Suez Canal. Mr. Fowler dealt
tenderly with Mr. Stephenson's dicta, and was lenient
to Mr. Hawkshaw's cautious, yet compromising,
report on the Canal. His own opinion was that the
Canal would not pay unless a good deal of the Indian
and Chinese Cape traffic were diverted into it. Lord
Palmerston declared the Canal ought not to be made.
Mr. Stephenson said it could not be made. Mr. Hawkshaw averred it could not be finished in the estimated time, and at the estimated cost. Mr. Fowler
declares it can be made at the estimated time and
cost; that Lord Palmerston's objections have been
met by recent changes in the relations of the
Company to the Egyptian Government; that Mr.
Stephenson's opinion is to be regretted; that Mr.
Hawkshaw's is erroneous; but that the Canal will
not pay, unless there is something more than mail
and passenger traffic to go through it, in addition
to the trade which it may create for itself.

At 1 o'clock we halted at Sonhadj, where the
vessels coaled, and the Prince went out shooting, but
got no sport. There was a very small dahabeah
here flying the United States flag, and apparently
laden with "notions" of various kinds; and some

distance farther on, we met a Britisher, going down
the river, which left Cairo two months ago. The
inhabitants were drawn up in rows at the landing-
place, where the officials were in waiting, with a
staff of cavasses in line to keep the little boys in
order; and at 2.30 P.M. the flotilla was off again.
At 4.20 P.M. passed Misneah, and, hugging the
right bank, made way against the strong current
which sweeps at the base of the great crags, rising
in well defined strata to a height of 300 or 400
feet above us. At one spot a body of dromedary
cavalry came down to serve as escort in case of
need—some fifteen or eighteen men—very wild and
picturesque-looking fellows, with long guns and
pistols in their belts; but they were headed off by
a projecting cliff, dived into a cleft in the mountain chain, and we saw them no more. The course
of the stream is carefully marked out by boughs of
palms and long feathery waving reeds stuck on the
shallows; boats, with shouting crews, moored at
difficult places; and watchmen who hail us from
the sand-banks and isolated shores of little islands.

At Girgeh, 341 miles from Cairo, which we
reached at 6.30 P.M., the fleet was put in shore-
wards and lay to for the night. The Governor
is one of the richest men in these parts, of an

ancient family, possessing a splendid house at Manfaloot, which is open to all travellers. A line
of fifty lanterns, suspended from a line of posts,
lighted up the landing-place. There was the usual
establishment of animated beacons, with their blazing
torches of pine-wood in iron hoops at the end of
long poles. Tents were pitched on an open space
by the river-banks, outside the town, at which there
was to have been an entertainment of music and
dancing-girls; but they were sent away, as it was
not possible to endure either the singing or the
dancing. Hundreds of men and boys assembled round
the fires and the blazing beacons, and sat on the
banks far into the late evening; but it is observable
that, whether from fear of the cavasses, or natural
good manners, they did not crowd round the Prince's
ship, and stare into the windows, which were ablaze
with wax-candles and gilded mirrors. What a contrast
to that crowd at Wimbledon, which no force of arms,
or threats, or prayers, could restrain from mobbing
the Sultan! When the Prince went on shore for a
few moments, there was a considerable gathering
of the people, but they did not press upon or in-
commode him, and many of those who came nearest
belonged to the flotilla itself. Our ever-joyous captain, Achmet Hassan, came on board to dinner, and

was as quick and entertaining as ever. Fourteen years
at sea, poor man! ere he had a little taste of shore
life. Yet he prefers the sea to Nile navigation. "I
never go down all day now — paddle-box, always
paddle-box,—shouting Fulley speed! Halfey speed!
Turney-stern! At sea, give my course to officer—
lie down, go sleep. Sea much better." Ali Risa
pointed out a passage in Lady Duff Gordon's Letters which he was reading, as a proof of bad taste.
It related to the Prince of Wales's marriage. Omar,
her servant, was represented to have asked when the
Prince "would see his wife's face," which Ali Risa
regarded as indelicate. So the Captain to-night, in
giving a general invitation to his house at Cairo,
on our return, said, "I will show you everything
—everything—only" (he smiled with all his white
teeth) "not my wife."

"But," said the Duke, "when you come to me
in Scotland, you will see the Duchess."

"Each country has its customs. If I take my
wife to Scotland, I let you see her face."

The Captain says he has only one wife; and then
he taps his breast and laughs, and adds, "I am
Englishman—one wife—one wife."

There has been a difficulty between our vessel and
Colonel Stanton's ever since we started; and a

want of good faith in the matter of milk, meat,
and provisions generally, is reciprocally attributed
to the Commissariat department. When the two
steamers come alongside, the cackle of the poultry
in the pens, and the gobbling of the turkeys on
the paddle-boxes, is quite overpowered by the animated outburst of speech in which Virgilio, Giovanni,
Attilio, Giacomo talk all together to Guiseppe and
Filippo, Geronimo and Baptiste, over the side. One
of our waiters, going on board the Consular boat
to indulge in the charming gabble so dear to Italian
servitori, was ejected by the Captain. Great wailing,
and a complaint to Ali Bey. An explanation is called
for. The Captain makes it clear that the Italian
was in undress, and could not be identified as a
person entitled to come on board, but recalls the
expulsion and manual application. Honour is satis-
fied, and peace is restored between Captain and man
by an affectionate salute on the cheek. A case of
champagne was opened last night sine permissu
superiorum, and three bottles were abstracted. Our
Captain infers that it must be Christians who did so,
"because," observes he, logically, "my crew all Mussulmen—Mussulmen only drink water." Perhaps so.

February 14th.—Left Girgeh at sunrise—such
a sunrise!—a cloudless sky, still studded with

twinkling stars in the deep blue of the far west,
while the east was glowing with orange and amber.
The sunrise in Egypt, at this time of year, is
rather colourless — too white, owing to a want of
watery clouds in the sky. A very fine morning,
nevertheless; wind firm, NE., fresh, but not keen
or chest-searching; and a sun which gained in power
every hour. There is a sharp look-out for crocodiles; but the Reis says it is in vain, for the
water is too cold and the air is not warm enough;
yet Sir S. Baker holds, that when the water
is cold and the sun is as bright as it is now,
crocodiles come out—or should do so. But they do
not. The Governor of Girgeh, if rightly interpreted,
declared that a crocodile had not visited the neigh-
bourhood for the last sixty years! But we have
passed the place where Lord H. Scott shot a beast,
according to Hamed, and where the Prince saw
many when he was last here.

After breakfast lay to off the right bank below
Farshoot for a time, having passed all that
remains of a large town, the rest of which will
soon, in all likelihood, follow into the bed of
the Nile. The tenacity with which the people
cling to the banks of the river, in spite of awful
warnings and constant depositions, is curious.

As we lay to the dahabeah Feodalinda, with
British colours, swept down with the stream, firing
a little salute from all her armoury, with three
Britishers standing, with heads uncovered, on deck.
To us it was a day of rest and thankfulness. To the
poor fellahs who were toiling by the river banks, only
to be distinguished from it in colour by the cloths
round their loins, and their head-pieces of felt, the
shadoof gives no rest from sunrise to sunset. Friday
—their Sabbath—brings them no repose. It is said
that there is a great scarcity to be feared from the
want of water in the Nile, and that the Viceroy is
making preparations to meet it by extensive purchases of corn—for he is not a political economist.
He does not understand the principles of free
trade as they were applied to a certain country in
1846. The approach to Keneh is indicated by
the rafts of water-jars—some many thousands in
number—floating down the river. On the right
great fields of water-jars lay on the beach; and, on
nearing the town, a group of six white cylindrical
windmills, with extinguisher-shaped tops, mark the
hill, or irregular plateau, beneath which the town is
situated. In the present state of the Nile it lies
some two miles away from the high bluff covered
with palm trees, and occupied by a native village,

by which the vessels were drawn up. There was
a crowd of turbaned sheiks waiting to do the Royal
party honour — the British Consular Agent, the
Deputy Governor of Esné, and many individuals of
repute in their way, with retinues of men, horses,
and asses—but it was too late to go to the town.
The Prince, however, accepted an invitation to the
Consular Agent's for the evening to see a dance.

There might have been a serious accident on our
arrival here. The Mudir had caused a landing-place
to be erected on a platform of wood, which was
covered with turf and earth, so that the visitors
might walk from the deck of the vessels on shore.
Getting on shore is one of the events of the day,
and there is a rapid movement from the steamers as
soon as the planks are laid. Fortunately, there are
always adventurous young men ready to take the
first step. Some said that the steamer, on coming to,
gave the platform a shake; others averred there was
an original defect of weakness in its constitution.
Any way, as Lord Carington was bounding towards
the bank, a crash was heard, and he and the platform
tumbled down together, involving Mr. Montagu and
Prince Louis in part of the ruin. Lord Carington
fell into the Nile, but he soon scrambled up the
bank, dripping like a Newfoundland, and not a bit

the worse for his little immersion. It might have been a very awkward fall for the Princess, and for a time the Mudir was in great disfavour. But all's well that ends well.

There is bad news for the sportsmen. The Prince's dogs roam about in vain, and never have need to stiffen tail or arrest their course over the fields. There are no quails, and one gets tired of shooting pigeons, hawks, and weeny owls. When it was dark, Colonel Marshall and I went on shore, intending to see the fantasia at the Consular Agent's, and were immediately beset by an irresistible crowd of donkey boys. He is not quite a feather weight, and except a French giant at a station on the Suez Canal, and an awful negro who encountered us at one of our halts, the like of him in stature was not seen in Egypt. But what will not donkey boys dare? They seized on him as if he were a baby, and by sheer force and united efforts put him first on one donkey and then on another, according to the temporary success of opposing factions. In vain he frustrated their efforts by the simple expedient of putting his feet on the ground, and letting the delighted donkey walk away from between his legs. They returned to the charge again and again. The night was hot, and the climate exhausting, and the

donkey boys were legion. I succumbed after a brief
struggle, and sat watching from my saddle a crowd
revolving in the dust, amidst which F. M. now
upreared his huge bulk in spite of himself, now
descending to the earth, striking out like a steam
hammer, till, worn out and defeated, he called for
help I could not give, and was led off in triumph
towards Kench. I followed, and as soon as we were
fairly disposed of, the crowd melted away, and left
us to some six or seven of the victors, who goaded
the animals into a gallop through the village, rousing
up all the dogs to madness by their cries. Suddenly
there darted out of a grove the most prodigious-
looking ruffian we had ever seen—Frenchman, negro,
British cuirassier, all were dwarfs to him—and as
he rushed down, whirling a six-foot staff shod with
iron, I instinctively clapped my hand on my revolver,
and F. M. exclaimed, " Did you ever see such a
scoundrel in your life?" My revolver was of course
in its case in the cabin, but the apparition meant
no harm. It turned out afterwards he was only the
village watchman. But, quis custodiem custodiet?
Watching an opportunity, I plucked his staff out of
his hand, and, to make assurance doubly sure, handed
it to F. M., who held it with iron grip, and gave it
an occasional flourish over the owner's head, whose

P

feelings were not too deep for words, for he yelled hideously. With him in our train, we pricked over the plain in the dusk, crossed the dry bed of a branch of the Nile, and entered the town, which was like any other town in Egypt. We were guided to the scene of a fantasia by the dub-a-dub of the drums, and the noise of voices, and dismounted at a door surrounded by a crowd of people. The court inside was crammed with turbans, and the heat was smothering. The stairs leading up from the court to the first floor of the Consular mansion were equally thronged. As we entered, a black servitor made us understand he wanted to announce us, and a great fear fell on us too. We had not been invited! Nor had we been introduced to the Egyptian gentleman who was good enough to take on himself to represent the power of Great Britain and Ireland at Keneh. Moreover, we had seen and heard enough, for some of the dancers were visible at the doorway, and the music beat full on our ear. And so we mounted and fled, just as Ali Risa came charging down to bear us to the presence. Fled, but not far or long. Flop! down came F. M. and his donkey in the dust, and, once there, the latter refused to rise, and my quadruped evinced a strong tendency to follow his example. The donkey boys were not in

the least put out. Making for the first house at
hand, one opened a door, and in a moment emerged,
leading forth a hapless ass, which had fondly believed
its work was over for the night. But out came the
owner too! And then such a clamour of words
arose! In the midst of the controversy we cantered
off, just as the principal inhabitants were coming out
to engage in the dispute, and steering our course
through the intricate channels of the narrow lanes,
reached the plain at last, and had a most delightful
ride in the moonlight, which was asserting its
supremacy, back to our steamer. The watchman was
quite happy at the restoration of his staff, and at the
receipt of a small gratuity; and in order to assert his
office and compensate himself for his temporary loss
of dignity and power, he hit a donkey boy, who was
doing nothing whatever, a smart tap on the skull
with the iron end. The Almeahs, or dancing-girls
of Kench, are celebrated for their beauty—by the
natives. They are exceedingly like British gipsy
women of an ordinary type, but they do not bear
such a good reputation. Here is a portrait of the
fairest of them, who was not, however, so famous a
dancer as a stumpy little woman, who had acquired
the art of vibrating her person from the breast to
the hips, whilst the rest of her body was motionless,

to a degree which is considered perfection. There
is one mistake in the sketch. The dancer should
not have shoes.

February 15th.—(Kench.) In the morning the
Princess made her first acquaintance with an
Egyptian Temple. True, it is 1,800 years old—quite
a modern affair. True, it is so highly ornate that
real antiquaries do not think much of it; but surely
it is something to gaze on the portrait of Cleopatra,
and to see the name of her son by Julius Cæsar
carved in solid rock while they were still alive, as fresh
as though it were done yesterday. It is something
to wander through courts where Roman legionaries

came from afar to worship the Egyptian Venus.
To the Royal party, at all events, the ancient
Temple and the neighbouring ruins were full of
deep interest. The Temple was cleared some years
ago by order of Mahomet Bey, but the sand appears
to be accumulating once more.

After breakfast, the steamers crossed over to the
other side of the river, and we set out to visit
Dendera, which, in the present state of the Nile, is
about two miles from the shore. The Prince mounted
a horse belonging to the Viceroy's son, and the
Princess rode her own milk-white and noisy donkey.

The critics may talk as they please. They may
call the figures "graceless," and abuse the "over-
charged capitals;" they may style the columns
"barbarous," an they list, but I am ignorant
enough to agree with Belzoni, and to confess my
admiration of this grand ruin—the most perfect,
it is said, of any in Egypt. "But," say the
Egyptologues, "that very perfection is a defect!
The long dead wall outside is hideous. When
rifted and broken, the beauty of a temple is
really seen." Here is a building of massive masonry, finished exquisitely, 220 paces long, by 50
paces broad, with a grand portico on twenty-four
giant columns, 25 feet round and 40 feet high,

opening on columned chambers and halls engraved
like a watch, older than any Christian temple
in the world. The capitals are ornamented with
women's heads with the ears of a cow. And
it is too rich, and too new, and too perfect for
the antiquaries! These Ptolemies were mere
mushroom nobodies. It is nothing that this
Temple was built on the site of an edifice erected
by Cheops himself. There was an offensive zodiac
on the ceiling of the portico, which is enough
to damn the whole place, for it is not Egyptian
at all! It is now safe in Paris. Then there are
Greek inscriptions! And Aulus Avilius Flaccus, as
prefect of the time, Aulus Fulvius Crispus, Com-
mander-in-Chief, and Sarapion Trychambus, Commandant of the district, have had the audacity
to record their names as the dedicators of the
Temple to the very great goddess Aphroditè,
whom the Egyptians called Athor, in the reign of
Tiberius, when he was ordering the whole world
to be taxed! The portraits of Cleopatra, I admit,
are disappointing; but who has seen a satisfactory
likeness of Mary Queen of Scots? And this was
cut in hard stone. The face and figure are marred
by time, and so are those of Cæsarion, her son by
the great Julius; who certainly ought to have

made a mark in the world, had he lived, and
possessed any hereditary favours. Near the Temple
of Athor there is another, very small, containing
three chambers only. On the wall is cut the
semblance of the Sacred Cow; and it is related
that when the Sepoys who came to Egypt with
our Expedition from India, which landed on the
shores of the Red Sea, and marched by the old
route to Kench, visited the place, they all fell on
their faces and worshipped the emblem. The whole
building is full of interesting details.

Another building still remains, and I shall
leave it to antiquarians to decide whether it is a
" lying-in " place or not—the building where
Athor was confined, or a temple in honour of her
child. Then there is a wide waste of ruins—
walls, columns in various stages of decay, blocks
of stone; slabs, all covered with hieroglyphs, portraits, emblems—the hawk, which is the Sun, with
the Beginning and the End, Iris, and Nephthys,
by its side; myriads of figures and signs in
stone; a propylon of the grandest character, to
which the Arch of Triumph, not to speak of Temple
Bar, must yield—and its fellow in fragments.
And Tentyris is a heap of rubbish — all that
is left some heaps of brick and rubble; and its

courtier chiefs, who worshipped the divine Tiberius,
son of god Augustus, have left but their monumental
flatteries behind them. In addition to the sand
and time, there have been two agencies at work
to deface these magnificent temples. With labour
villanously laborious, the brutalized Mahometan
has worked at the destruction of every face and
likeness on the walls, too often successfully, and
always leaving his indelible mark. Then myriads
of rascally bees, which make no honey, but appear
to be able to perforate solid stone, have constructed
cities which look as hard as the very rock, on
the outer walls of the Temple, covering over
inscriptions and images with an armour which no
one dare pierce. Professor Owen took rather an
interest in them, but his researches were terminated
by a disposition on their part to take an interest
in him. It was the prettiest picture possible to
see the Princess wandering about the ruins—to
watch her tracing out the features, with the aid
of a cane, of stony Cleopatra on the wall.
What a contrast between our fair mistress and the
Serpent of Old Nile! For hours the party wandered here and there, and the hum of voices
aroused up the bats and hawks in the recesses of
the ruins. A fire was kindled, and the repast was

spread in the shade of the portico; and the
chibouquejees appeared with diamond-studded pipes
and jewelled coffee-cups, when lunch was over;
and we reposed for a time out of the heat, in
the cool of the Temple. The thermometer marked
73° even there.

Then, after a grateful rest, the word was "To
horse" (read donkey passim please), and returning
to the steamers, sated with the wonders of Tentyris,
Prince and Princess and their following embarked,
and were on their way towards Thebes ere the sun
had sunk behind the solemn ruins. The flotilla
passed the site of Coptos, destroyed by Diocletian.
This was, says Sir Gardner Wilkinson, the mart of
Indian commerce. There were once temples here,
attributed to Thotmes and to kings of the eleventh
dynasty. The early Christians pulled down these
temples to build them a church. That church has
now disappeared.

Then darkness menaced our timid captains. The
Soudan—Fezegoloo—for them if mishap comes to
Prince or Princess! So they draw up to the shore
and make fast at no place in particular. There
is a village some way off—Hamed says its name
is El Arabat. The El Arabatites were rather astonished when the party landed from the steamers

and commenced a brisk fusillade against all volatile creatures till it was too dark to see. The Prince seems to be the best shot of the "société," for no amount of loyalty will induce a man to go on missing for ever. In compliment to the genius loci of Tentyris, who had a great enmity to the sacred crocodile, eager search was made along the river banks for the interesting reptile, but he might as well have been looked for between Putney and Richmond.

CHAPTER IX.

"WE shall be at Thebes in the morning!" Our
last word at night. And Hamed, who has just said
his prayers in the moonlight—why I know not, for
we thought three times a day was the proper and
complete complement of devotion required of the
most devout of Moslem—says, "Taybe a very nice
place; all old ruin about made by King Solomon, de
say." I have forgotten to tell you who Hamed is,
though he has been mentioned more than once.
When the Duke was waiting at Cairo for Prince
and Princess, he was assailed by people who wished
to be engaged as dragoman for his party on the
Nile. One, highly recommended, a Syrian gentleman
in spectacles, very nearly established himself. He
would leave remuneration to our noble selves. It
would do when we all returned. Whatever we gave
would be enough. But he was asked to préciser

himself, and to do it in writing. So he sent in an
estimate. At first it was supposed he was under
the idea that he was to provide food and drink for
all the party, and he was told we were the Viceroy's
guests, and that everything was paid for on board
the steamer. But he held fast to his figures, and
merely remarked that he "would like to pay de
donkey boy very handsome—just for the noble
Duke sake." When he was derided and rejected,
he came down some hundred per cent., but was still
soaring high in regions of the impossible. Finally
rejected, he did not despair of his prey, but came
out on us in the form of an antiquarian—"De most
lubly dings in Egypt. No one else hab them. Je
vous jure, altesse! Cléopadre's neglace! I find her
myself!" How he haunted our doorsteps and sat in
our halls! But one day Hamed turned up, and he
was at once secured. Do you remember the stout,
short, jolly person who waited on the hippopotami
long ago in the Zoological Gardens, and who, from
association with them, had become almost hippopo-
tamic in expression—dark-skinned, dark-eyed, sleek,
and round? This was "Hippopotamus Johnny."
He came to England with the first little river-horse
—"all de same as my leetle child"—leaving his old
mother somewhere up in Nubia, in the parts near

Khartoum; and he has since been dragoman for "de long Desert caravan jerney." A devout man is Hamed, and very honest, I think, and very slow. He forgives even the hippopotamus all the wrong it did him. "When I go wid de leetle calf he boder me very troublesome. He go into him wash baat in ship; den him come out all wet—smell about for Hamed, and roll me about wid him damp big nose. I get no sleep—so says captain, 'I make you sleep in hammick;' and he sling one in de house where me and de calf wor. De first night I get in de hammick when de calf in him water, and I hear him come back, and smell—smell—all over for me: round he go, and grunt, and grunt, and sniff. Then I laugh to myself. Not long I laugh! Helo! my face is grinded up agen de cabin top, and my eye flash de fire and my nose he bleed. De leetle rascal calf, he got up on him hind leg, and give me a great dig wid him big snout, and knock hammick and all agen de roof, and near kill me. I wor very fond of him, to be sure!" And Hamed was engaged as dragoman, and found us more troublesome, I fear, even than his fat friend.

The whole party were awake early. We saw the Princess and Mrs. Grey were on the deck of their boat, and the Prince soon came up and joined

them. But the river is not very interesting just
here, for the valley is wide and low; though on our
right the hills of the Desert rise abruptly to a considerable height over the plain in which lie perdu
from us the Memnonium and the Colossi. On our
left is Karnak, and there, beyond, is Luxor, to which
we are tending—the Thebes in general of the tourist.
Alas! that one must speak or write of what we
saw! Words! words! words! How that grandeur
mocks you! But here we are at Luxor. The
flotilla arrived at 9 o'clock.

It was intensely hot. The travellers' boats moored
below the ruins were covered in with sun-shades.
Nor did many of the English, Russians, and
Americans — whose nationality was indicated by
standards flying—venture out to see the arrival of
the Royal party. But they kept up volleys of
fowling-pieces from their boats in sign of welcome,
and a small gun on shore gave deeper volume to
the sound at irregular intervals.

From the summit of the ancient Temple, in
which Mustapha Aga, the British Consular agent,
has his dwelling, floated the flags of the United
States and of Great Britain, and the Austrian,
French, and Russian banners were displayed from
various points, in company with the Ottoman

standard. The boats were hung with palm-branches, lemons, and oranges, and on the bank of the river the principal people of the place were assembled to receive the Royal party. By-and-by I shall try to say a word of Luxor itself, but now I must take the order of events as it came.

Mustapha Aga—who, next to the ruins, is perhaps the best-known "object" about Thebes—went on board to pay his respects. His feelings during the Mason and Slidell controversy must have been of a distracting character, for he is Consul for Great Britain and Consul for the United States, and hoists the flag of the one, and over his door is the escutcheon of the arms of the other. The Prince landed, and proceeded to his house to see the collection of curiosities, and a wonderful mummy, which looks as fresh as if Mustapha Aga and his family had just given it the last coat of paint and gilding.

I wish no harm to Mustapha, but I should like very much to pull his house down, not about his ears, but from between the ruins in which it stands. It is planted up there like a swallow's nest against the eave of a Greek temple. There was a haie of twenty or thirty Europeans between the river bank and Mustapha's porch, and a screen of reeds and festoons was erected outside for the little procession

which the Princess with Mrs. Grey headed from the
steamers. Pipes and coffee were of course brought
in, when mummy and scarabæus had been examined;
and outside there was congregated a mass of donkey
boys, and some good horses, led by syces. As we
saw afterwards, there was a large gathering of natives
not two hundred yards away—market-day at Luxor.
But indolence, ignorance, or indifference—what you
will—its influence was so great, not one ever stirred
to inquire into the cause of the firings and general
tomasha.

About midday the Prince and Princess started
for Karnak, magnâ comitante catervâ. And a very
pretty procession it was—the Princess on her milk-
white ass, caparisoned in red velvet and gold, and
the Prince on an animal of the same kind, of
darker hue. The donkey is the favourite beast of
the saddle. The horse is generally fidgety, head-
tossing, much neighing, given to ground and lofty
tumbling, which in a hot sun and on broiling sand
is not conducive to comfort. There were Mrs.
Grey, the Duke of Sutherland, Prince Louis of
Battenberg, the Marquis of Stafford, Lord Albert
Gower, Lord Carington, Colonel Marshall, Mr.
Montagu, Professor Owen, Mr. Fowler, Mr. Sumner,
Sir H. Pelly, Colonel Stanton, Sir S. Baker, Dr.

Minter, Major Alison, Mourad Pasha, Abd-el-Kader
Bey, Ali Risa, Mr. Brierly, Mr. George, and myself, with a preceding and surrounding of chibouquejees, syces, guides, cavasses, dragomans—
conspicuous among them the gorgeous Hadji Ali,
Colonel Stanton's dragoman, and Hamed—a gay
crowd on horses and asses, cantering, in clouds of
dust—all bright with fantastic dresses, turbaned, and
loose-robed—in a long stream, over irrigated land
and sandy desert; now spreading out like a fan of
many colours, again condensed in an undulating
cord-like file over the plain. And so, chatting and
laughing, out from Luxor to the waste where once
trod many myriad feet—Mustapha Abd-el-Kader and
Sir S. Baker wheeling and whirling, according to their
skill, in the wild pleasures of jereed play, which, considering that the sun was excessively powerful and
burning, did not commend itself largely to our party.
Our Italian and French domestics and the Turkish
chibouqueaille always attend on these occasions,
and the brawny sailors of the Ariadne career gloriously on steed or ass, and emulate the hippodamic
chibouquejees. And wherever the Prince goes the
faithful Downie is sure to be; nor is Peter Robertson far off, nor the guardian of the Prince's gun.
Alister, of course, is ever with the Duke. We are

going all wrong, of course. We should visit the ruins
on the left bank of the Nile first, and finish with
Luxor. I do not think it matters much. Certainly
it did not affect any of the party around the Royal
travellers, and never were more joyous, light-hearted
people en route to Karnak. Some two hundred
people, perhaps, all in full cry, and merry as the
morn. And the solemn grandeur of the ruined
Temples came on us at last!

Well! It is in the idea of "what must have
been" that much of the impression produced by
these ruins is based. They are the only works of
human hands I know of which produce the effect of
awe. The immense antiquity of what we see affects
us only in relation to that fact. Any stone at our
feet is older by countless ages. But our fellow-men
hewed these blocks and built them up, and drew
those figures and cut those emblems in the nonage of
the world. There is a god-like grandeur in the
labours of these poor, nameless multitudes. Time
has cast over them the shadow of eternity. What
lies before us seems superhuman, but only because no
human creature now can wield the power to which
these owe their erection. "What this must have
been!" That is the thought which fills the breast
with something like veneration as we walk down

what was once the Avenue of Sphinxes, now a rough
broad path in the Desert sand, covered with stones,
sand, fragments of slabs, flints, and lined formerly
by a border of gigantic Sphinxes at short distances,
of which not one remains complete. These Sphinxes
had the heads of rams, the neck and busts of women,
and the arms and claws of a lion. So much can be
gathered from an inspection of the colossal fragments
of the hundreds which cover the ground. They
were sedulous destroyers who did so much work here.
The avenue formed by these Sphinxes led to a gateway or Pylon which is still erect, and rises to the
height of 140 feet, its massive blocks recording that
it is the work of Ptolemy Euergetes, and Berenice
his wife, who are, according to our guide-book, represented making offerings to their predecessors and
parents. Ptolemy is said to be shown somewhere
in a Greek costume, but I could not make him out.

The Royal party, in irregular procession, approached the ruins by this Avenue of Sphinxes,
which is at the south-west entrance, and passing
through the Ptolemaic Pylon, made an examination
of the sculptured stones, most of them dismounting
and handing over the animals to the syces. Thence
they proceeded down a second avenue of mutilated
Sphinxes, by far older than the first, and passed

through a Pylon, 80 feet high, into a court, in which
one perfect column alone remains to show how
grand must have been the stupendous rows of its
fellows, the fragments of which are lying all around.
It is said to be near 90 feet high, and the remains
of twenty-five, of similar size, can be counted in
this court, which belongs to a Temple built by
Rameses III. and his successors, dating about 1200
B.C. A Pharaoh who preceded Shishak, the contem-
porary of Solomon, also had a hand in it.

I do freely avow how ignorant I am of the manner in which learned men work out their interpre-
tations, but, I believe. I remember long ago being
called on to accept it as a fact that the Latin word
"sylva," a grove, was derived from the Greek ὑλη,
and I did so. But what is to be thought of a dispute concerning a hieroglyph which, if I understand
aright, is translated by some as "Amyrtæus" and
by others as "Nectanebo"? M. Marriette avers that
if an inscription be sent to half a dozen eminent
scholars, they will agree in rendering it as readily as
if it were Greek or Latin, and with very slight dis-
crepancies. And see! there is Mr. Smith translating
passages for the Princess as fast as he can talk—and
that is pretty well. A thorough New Englander—
somewhere from Boston, I guess—pattering away

about Rameses and Osiris. It is well for the Smiths
that the Pharaohs are no more, for republican
manners might have led to unpleasant results. The
Prince and Princess were then conducted into the
great roofless Hall of the Palace built, according to
Lepsius, by Rameses II., the Pharaoh who lived in
the time of Moses, and dating, according to that
authority, 1380 years before Christ.

The Lepsius in question is not the learned person
mentioned by Mr. Shandy, who composed a work
the day he was born, but he is a recent travelled and
learned German, rather unjustly attacked for outrages
on the monuments of Egypt. Let all who visit
Luxor ask to see his very amusing and instructive
" Livre des Voyageurs." It begins with a hierogly-
phic title-page, in which it is recorded, in characters
taken from the monuments, with some modern adap-
tations, how Lepsius came out to Egypt under the
patronage of the King of Prussia. Then there is a
very learned, and yet light dissertation, on Egyptian
history and antiquities, and an exposé of the purpose of the book, which is, that travellers may record
observations in it—a very useful purpose—making in
time the volume a valuable record. And the sugges-
tion has been treated with marked neglect. Some
recommend their dragoman; others try to express, in

various languages, poetical inflations about Thebes and Karnak. One Britisher has discovered a curious cartouch, which he commends to Dr. Lepsius. It is copied in the book, and looks very like a "donkey eating thistles!"

To return to the Hall—the grandest work in the world. It stands in the centre of a court, 278 feet long by 329 broad, which is bordered by covered corridors, with a double row of columns in the centre leading to the Hall. There are advanced towers or propyla to this enclosure, and our guide-book states that the lintel-stones of the doorway want only two inches of 41 feet in length. The stones of the ceiling are of equal size, every one covered with sculptures or paintings. In the centre there are twelve columns of incomparable grandeur, 70 feet high, with plinth and abacus, and 33½ feet in circumference; and in rows parallel to these are no less than 126 columns, 42½ feet high and 28 feet round, in seven rows of nine columns each. One column in this hall was presented in almost a miraculous condition. Shaken by an earthquake, or undermined by the overflow of the Nile, it had fallen against its neighbour, so that the entablature rested against the side, and thus the whole mass was upheld at an acute angle, although it is composed of a num-

ber of great stones, which seem held together by
magic. The doorways are stupendous. There are
towers before each.

Passing out of this court, we came upon two obelisks, one of which has been overthrown, and broken
into several pieces, and then upon another court, with
two obelisks, one in a similar condition, the other
still erect, and measuring 94 feet in height. The
party was now lost in labyrinths of ruin—enormous
blocks of stone, broken columns, shattered pillars,
granite, limestone, and sandstone, alike in pieces.
The Sanctuary—a building of red granite, erected by
a Pharaoh, destroyed by Cambyses, and rebuilt by
Philip—the pillars and columns of a Temple erected
by Thotmes III.—Alexander's Hawk—and ruins
again fill up the remainder of the vast area, which is,
measured, one and a half English miles. Persians
and Greeks, Cambyses and Ptolemy, have done their
worst, and man built up that man might destroy.
The Nile aids time in completing the work. The
base of the columns and pillars is covered with
nitrous salts, left by the waters of inundation, and
I scraped off some which burnt in paper like salt-
petre. As to the sculptures on the walls, nothing but
an immense series of photographs can give the least
idea of them. War is the chief subject—the vic-

tories of Osiris.   There is a bridge over the Nile to
be remarked, but the works of peace are few.   One
compartment is interpreted as the representation of
the conquests of Shishak, in his expedition against
Jerusalem.   In another place there are traces of early
Christians, who selected the ruins as abiding refuges.

The Prince and Princess explored recesses and
chambers, and wandered about the ruins at will, the
party breaking up into little knots of independent
explorers.   They had the advantage of being accompanied by Mr. Smith, who had his own expla-
nations to offer of the sculptures.   The sun was
very hot, and the thermometer stood at 104° inside
the ruins—at least so a Celsius, which a philosophical lady brought with her, was made to read.
But a shady place was found for lunch, in the
vast colonnade of the Great Hall.   Carpets were
spread, and the resources of the providore were
displayed in the feast, to which the Prince invited
a Russian officer—Count Gerbel—and his wife.   The
effect of the streaks of sunshine which fell through
the rifted walls and colossal columns on groups of
Egyptians, Arabs, Turks, Arnaouts, and guides,
gathered about the horses and donkeys in the Great
Hall, and on the various coated, booted, hatted, and
knickerbockered Europeans, was very picturesque.

The latter certainly must astonish the natives at
times by their costumes. Peter Robertson, the
Highland piper, has invented a particularly ingenious adaptation of his kilted attire to the latitude
in which he is travelling.

We not unwillingly rested in the grateful shade,
whilst the servants laid out the banquet, which
would have astonished even Rameses in all his glory.
Then there were pipes and coffee and conversation,
and a brief repose; and when every one was refreshed
we proceeded in the Royal train to the southern
gate of the open court, at the side of which is an
inscription (said to be) concerning an eclipse of the
sun; visited the temple dedicated by Alexander to
his father Philip; thence, past the well which
supplied the defenders of the fortifications, to the
palace of Thotmes III., and to another court,
in which lie many mutilated statues.

Remounting, the Prince and Princess and their
following returned to Luxor as they came, and
went over the Temples, which are close to the Nile,
and form part of the town. They carefully examined
the monuments, in spite of the heat and dust.

We were sated with ruin, and the works of Amunoph and Rameses began to pall. But how stately
and how vast they are! What would it not be worth

to behold, at one coup d'œil, the surpassing grandeur
of the scene which must have been presented here when
the Temples and Palaces were perfect, and when from
Luxor the priest-kings in all their glory proceeded
along the sphinx-guarded avenues, right away to
glorious Karnak, to celebrate feast, or rite, or victory?
Here are temples built by Amunoph III., 1450 B. C.
— a mass of columns and sculptured stones —
sanctuaries and chambers. They are plastered and
bewattled to turn them into dwelling-places for the
Arabs, and we disturbed families of goats, children
and old women in their homes as we trod the halls of
the Pharaohs. Hovels of the vilest, and huts of mud
crowd the bases of the walls and pillars. There is
another grand work—a Temple and gateway—with a
façade 200 feet long and 60 feet high, on the side of
which are sculptured the exploits of Rameses II. the
Great, son of Sesostris. What are we to say of the
Abyssinian Expedition, when we look at the records
of this monarch's victories in Asia and India, in the
fourteenth century before Christ? Two prodigious
statues of red granite still guard the gateway, all de-
faced and buried in sand and rubbish. One of the
servants of the ship chipped off a piece of his nose
as a souvenir! The granite has yielded to time,
and falls away in flakes at a slight touch.

Can nothing be done by the civilized nations of
the world together to preserve Karnak and Luxor?
All nations have a common interest in the preservation of these magnificent monuments. They are in
great danger. The Nile menaces them every year,
and it would need very little to cause the fall of
many a glorious pillar which a very little outlay could
render safe. And as to man. He ruins what he
cannot remove very often, and what he removes
is placed in museums, which may be rifled and
ransacked by conquest in time to come.

At the Prince's desire, preparations were made to dig
down to the base of the Great Obelisk, companion to
that in the Place de la Concorde, which was presented
to Great Britain. Mr. Smith stated, there were two
gigantic asses at the base of the obelisk, but it was
not found that they were in the place he indicated.
It is vain to express a wish for the removal of what
belongs to us, I suppose. The non-user of our right
has led to doubts of its existence; and Colonel Stanton had a sharp controversy with Mourad Pasha, who
denied that the Obelisk belonged to us at all.

It was 5 o'clock when we returned to the shade
of the awnings of the steamers, and of all the party
the Princess, who had seen most, seemed the least
fatigued. At night the flotilla was illuminated, the

dahabeahs were hung with lanterns, and the river glittered with the reflection of hundreds of fires. Blue lights were burnt, and there was a rivalry between Woolwich and Egypt in the flights of rockets which flew hissing into the serene, bright-starred sky. The avenue of palm-branches and the façade of Mustapha's house were illuminated also, and blazing beacons bordered the bank of the river. Native boats floated down to the music of wild choruses, and vanished in the darkness.

The day and night were equally worthy of remembrance. On board the Prince's ship there was a dinner of more than usual state, and Mr. Smith was invited to the Royal table, in addition to the Russian Count and others.

February 17th.—To-day was devoted to a visit to the "Valley of the Kings," on the left (or west) bank of the river, one of the most interesting excursions in the world. Sixty or seventy horses and donkeys were collected for the party, which was transported at 10 o'clock to the other side, lower down the Nile. The news of the coming had gone abroad, and, in addition to the usual gathering of syces, servants, and retainers, there was an assemblage of natives, who seemed to have come out of the Desert. Crowds of Arab children, boys and girls, kept up with us the

whole way to the Valley, carrying pitchers of water,
and others presented "antiques" for sale at all points
of the route—timid persistent creatures, full of desire
to please and to secure baksheesh.   The kindness
of the Prince and Princess to these little people on
the way soon made them favourites, and secured for
them rather too much attention.   His Royal Highness has taken a fancy to a little soft-eyed, white-
toothed lad, named Yousouf, who follows his donkey,
and wants to take him to England.   Yousouf is in
great perplexity of mind on the subject.   The long
hot ride to the Valley terminated only that the exploration of the Tombs of the Kings might begin;
and Prince and Princess dismounted in a blazing
sun, and set to work under the guidance of Mr.
Smith, who is in grand "concurrence" with Mustapha Aga.   It was a very trying day.

Deep into the earth the Prince and Princess dived,
among broken slabs and rough stones, examining the
chambers of the dead, where painted records and
engraved stones preserve the memory of the deeds of
the departed tenants to those who can decipher them.
Belzoni's tomb, Bruce's tomb, and two others were
explored.   The Princess bore the heat and the rough
ascents and descents with indefatigable good-will and
enterprise.

This was a day of lamentation for me. Some way or other, the note-book I had been sedulously filling all the way dropped out of my pocket in clambering about the tombs. When the loss was made known, although a great reward was offered to the finder, the knowing ones shook their heads. Colonel Stanton, and Mr. Smith, and Mustapha Ali Risa agreed that the chances were much against me. The reason was this,—" If an Arab found it, he would keep it and hide it, lest he should be accused of stealing it!" What a commentary on the treatment of the people! They have no faith in the European, because he is of the race, they think, which governs them, and thus they act so as to deserve their old traditional character, and cause every man's hand to be against them. "Years hence," said Ali Risa, and with him agreed all the dragomanry, " that pocket-book will be offered to some traveller as an antica found in the Tombs, and then the Arab will be horrified at getting a kick, or a stick, or being laughed at for his pains." And they were right. The sum I offered set every one pretending to look for the book, but no one found it. An Arab must have pounced on it at once, as it fell.

One sees too much in a day to remember all
distinctly. The head becomes filled with pylons
and propylons, sphinxes, columns, obelisks, hieroglyphs, as confused and broken up and jumbled
as are the things themselves which have left the
impressions. But I recollect well enough that it
seemed the most interesting sight possible to watch
the young travellers, on whose future there are such
vast interests depending, moving about among the
poor Arabs in the gloom of these terrible
mortuary chambers, and trying to decipher the
records left thousands of years ago of their lives
and exploits by other Royal personages, on the
walls. Bab-el-Molook is a wonderful place indeed.
Desolate, exceedingly; an arid valley of stone,
rock, and mountain, burnt by the sun, without
tree, or blade of grass, or green thing. Such it
could not have been when the kings of Thebes
chose it as the site of the subterranean City of
the Dead; for the approaches, at least, were like
the barren plain on which the Memnonium and
the Colossi are placed; then, doubtless, cultivated
—covered with trees and residences.

It would be wrong to say no living thing is to
be found in this valley. The rocks swarm with
scorpions, many of which were captured and bottled

off. What form of insect life the horrors feed upon
I cannot say. These, and a few outcast sand-martens
flitting about at the entrance to the Valley, were all
I could see outside the Tombs. Inside there were
bats, which shows that there must be insects about
at night; and once, as Alison and I were groping
down the shaft-like entrance to one of the tomb
galleries, candle in hand, something dark flew with a
clatter over the loose stones and vanished—jackal, fox,
or hyena. Deep in the solid rock, more than 3,200
years ago, Osiri, father of Sesostris, prepared the
home for the alabaster sarcophagus in which his
mummy was to rest; now, I think, installed in the
British Museum. Belzoni, the fame of whose tremendous size and strength still lives among the
Arab guides, was the modern discoverer of this
gallery, which now bears his name. It is 180 feet
below the surface, and to get at it you must first
descend a rough flight of broken steps cut in the
rock some thirty feet, which takes you to the first
landing from the top, and then go down a similar
flight which conducts you to the ground floor.
Here there is a passage which leads to a square
chamber—a sham—for the kernel of the nut lay
inside. Belzoni was not deceived, for he burst
through the wall, came upon a chamber with pillars,

descended from it to a chamber with two pillars,
went along two passages, entered another chamber,
found one still further on, and at last found himself
where we were standing, in a vaulted room, 20 feet
long and 30 feet wide, in which lay the plundered
sarcophagus described then as lying at the mouth
of a shaft cut at a slope into the rock for 150 feet,
with a flight of steps at either side. Amid these
chambers are smaller rooms and recesses in the
rock. We were now 320 feet from the entrance, and
there was, it may fairly be said, not a foot of the
walls or ceilings in all that course of gallery or
chamber which was not covered with paintings or
hieroglyphs on a sort of smooth plastered surface.
To give an account of these would be to write a
book, and a large one, which after all would be but a
dry catalogue "Bruce's Tomb," as it is called, which
was prepared by Rameses III. for himself and friends,
is 405 feet long, and the walls are a perfect history
and record of life in Egypt. These kings afforded
constant employment to their subjects, though I
suspect it was not highly remunerated; and they certainly must have been a trouble to their neighbours.
For centuries the Tombs have been visited by the
curious, and it is much to be regretted that instead of
recording their feelings about the objects they visited,

R

they did not tell us something about the people of
the time in the land in which they were travelling.
Thus we might have learned how the Egyptians
fared, and how they became what they are. Possibly
one of these visitors expressed the sentiments
towards the close of the day of some of our own
party. As Sir Gardner Wilkinson records, he wrote
as follows, in Tomb No. 9—that of Rameses V. :
Ἐπιφανιος ιστορησα ουδεν δε εθαυμασα η μη τον λιθον,
" Epiphanius saw nothing wonderful but the stone."
Mr. Epiphany has a large sect of philosophers of
his sort at the present time. The other tomb we
inspected was that of Pthamen-se-pthah. To visit
all would need a week; and there are more than
twenty of these tombs, if historians be correct,
which remain unopened to this day.

Her Royal Highness astonished the party by
indomitable spirit and resolution, in the full blaze
of an Egyptian sun, and by capacity to endure
fatigue. Those who looked far more able to go
through a long day's work, exploring mummy-caves,
and investigating dark catacombs, admitted the
Princess was much stronger. Her interest in what
she saw, and the delight which she manifested,
animated the Royal party.

The illumination of the Tombs by magnesium

wire torches produced the most beautiful effects,
though they were transient. One disagreeable result
was the excitement produced in the bat-world, the
citizens of which came swarming from dark corners
about the ears of the Royal party. Candles were
far more useful, as they enabled individuals to study
details at their leisure. At last we emerged finally
into the open day. And, lo! there was a tent
pitched at the mouth of a tomb; and there was a
strange sound heard outside, where the French
domestics of the Viceroy and the Prince's men are
preparing the feast. It was the churning of the
machine for making ice. The Turks were busy
making coffee. Hampers were unpacked, and camels
eased of their loads, and the Valley of the Tombs
of the Kings resounded with voices. Lunch was
laid in the shade of the entrance to a tomb, No. 9,
Rameses within not objecting. Indeed, judging
from the subjects depicted on the walls of the cata-
comb, it would seem that the Pharaoh of 3,000 years
ago was not indifferent to creature comforts, though
soda-water and ice-making machines and French
wines were not known to him.

The sun had lost some of its power when we
started to return, but the heat in the Valley was
excessive; and one wondered if it were true that

Ibrahim Pasha led an army up through it on an expedition against some Arab troublesomes. It was even averred that a part of our Indian force proceeded some way in the uninviting road when they were in Egypt. Several of the gentlemen took the short way over the mountain crags at the side on foot, with Arab guides, and from the account they gave of the view of the Nile valley, and of Luxor on the opposite bank, and of the plain below, I was sorry I did not follow their example. It is a short cut to the river, which we reached and crossed half an hour ere sunset. The evening was so warm and calm that the Prince, with Lord Carington, Mr. Montagu, and Lord Stafford, took a boat across and bathed at the other side. Mustapha Aga gave a dance, which the Prince and suite and the Duke of Sutherland's friends attended; but the performance was not remarkable, and only one of the women, and she neither young nor good-looking, seemed inspired with the spirit of the ancient mystic dance of Egypt. They were all animated, however, by the modern Egyptian spirit as to baksheesh.

February 18th.—The two parties started early in boats across the river, and, taking horses and donkeys at the other side, rode to the end of the Assaseef, and to Deayr Bachree, where they examined

the beautiful frescoes, passing through and by numerous mummy catacombs, with the bodies and bones
lying exposed in all directions. When I say that
the Royal party to-day visited the ruins at Assasecf,
Koorneoh, Medeenet Haboo, Dayr-el-Medeeneh, and
the Memnonium, returning by the two Colossi and
the Vocal Memnon, those who are acquainted with
the ruins will admit that it was good work, performed
as it was in a sun only little less scorching than that
of yesterday. One of the least agreeable incidents
of our wanderings to-day, was the visit to the
mummy pits; or rather the evidences of destruction
and disregard for the dead which lay around us
on every side. The contents of the pits have been
dragged out, and skulls, with the hair still clinging
to the waxed cloth, legs, arms, jaws, ribs, were
scattered over acres of rock. Sometimes there was a
sickening odour, as though a slow decomposition
was still going on in the remains laid to rest thousands of years ago. The Arab children offered us
mummies of the Ibis and Scarabæi, objects taken
from the Tombs, and now and then pieces of bone
or earthen vessels full of parched corn.

It is impossible to convey an idea of them; but
every well-educated person has a conception of what
most of these ruins are like. Who has not seen the

Colossi and the Memnonium in sketch or engraving?
Whole books, very large and very learned, have been
devoted to the Thebaid and its remains; and for
many centuries in the old days of the ancient world,
ere the black night of barbarism put out the lamp of
learning, then flickering and feeble—for long genera-
tions, and ever since travel was practicable in the present ages of the world, the antiquarian and illuminati
had visited, to theorize, to wonder, and sometimes to
despoil. Stolid utilitarians regard these awful ruins
as evidences of the ignorance of those who reared the
records of their vanity and their faith, which have
defied the rage of man, and the tooth of time, and
the strife of the elemental forces—they are all so
many illustrations of "unproductive labour," exhausting capital and devouring a nation's strength.
Others measure the stones and calculate the weight
of the blocks, and start notions respecting the means
by which they were transported. Some are content
to see, admire, and deplore. The only way to get a
full idea of these remains is to live among them for
weeks, to pitch a tent and reside on the spot day
after day, with a few chosen companions, and to
explore at leisure site after site.

It is a thousand pities that in all the modern
world, with its wealth and resources, no organization

can be formed to clear away and explore the ruins,
guard and preserve what is left, and investigate what
yet remains hid.   The Viceroy is animated with the
best spirit.   But he has to deal with the living and
not with the dead.   He has to regenerate and resus-
citate Modern Egypt.   True there are guardians now
to the Temples, but they are ignorant and accessible
to influences.   It is a vain hope that some united
action of the European Powers, in the interests of
history, may be brought to bear on Egypt.   No one
who is acquainted with what has yet been done, can
hesitate to admit that enormous results might yet
be achieved in clearing away the clouds which hang
over the history of early civilization, by systematic
application of subsidized investigation.

I was very much struck, on my return to Cairo, by
the appearance of certain emissaries from the Prince
of Tigré in Abyssinia, who had come to the Viceroy
with presents.   In one of the catacombs of Koornet
there is a representation of black officers, said to be
of Cush or Ethiopia, offering gold rings, fans, and
cattle to Ammon Thun, a stranger king, who is identified with Amunoph III.   The men who came to the
Pharaoh of 1869 were like the ambassadors of the
land of Cush in face and dress, and they offered to
him gold rings and fans and ivory !

We got back to the steamer at 5.30 P.M. Abd el
Sultan Bey, Inspector General of the Upper Province,
joined the party on board the Royal steamer, and
in the evening there took place the great event
which marked the visit to Thebes. After dinner
the Prince and Princess and party landed, and, attended by a great crowd with lanterns and torches,
set out on donkeys and horses for the ruins of the
Temples of Karnak. The moon was only a few
days old, but still capable of casting strong shadow,
marking the outlines of the mounds of deserted
towns which lie outside Luxor. The more enter-
prising spirits dashed on ahead, and woke up the
night owls with imitations, for the most part rather
meritorious, of native war-cries. At last, the dim
outlines of the Great Ruin commanded silence.
Cantering on down the Avenue of Sphinxes, the
horsemen plunged into darkness, among the columns
of the Temple. Dim shapes became visible, and
presently a voice sang out, "This isn't the way
in. Put your head about, if you please." Colonel
Stanton, Sir S. Baker, with the men of the Ariadne,
and a band of Egyptian sailors, were before us,
preparing a surprise for the Princess. The horsemen turned and headed back the Royal procession,
which, seen afar over the plain, seemed like a

street full of lights taking a walk by itself, lamps
and all. They all turned down the Avenue of
Sphinxes, and the peasants in the village skirted
on their way must have felt a strange fear as they
heard the tramp of many feet, and saw the torch-
light which flashed through the chinks of their
humble dwellings. The party, dismounting outside
the Ruins, entered the solemn pile, and were left
to the light of the pale moon and of the watchful
stars which had so looked down on the priest-
kings—the Pharaohs—who built it thirty centuries
ago. Suddenly there came on us a blinding gleam
of intense whiteness from a recess in the ruin.
It grew in splendour and in power. The towering
columns of the portico, the plinths and obelisks,
grandiose blocks of carved stone, with all their
strange language in bird and beast, emblems,
secret histories, were revealed as if the sun had
burst on us out of the wall of hewn rock. What
a mass of pale faces there, shimmering ghostlike,
screening their eyes from the dazzling wonder!
What a hum of voices, swelling into a chorus of
admiration! As the Prince and Princess slowly
made their way up to the colonnade, the brilliant
wire, from column to column, casting the blackest
shadows, threw its rays like fixed lightning. They

reached the end of the Great Hall. Then blue, red, and green lights burned, and blazing torches, from broken pillar and heaped-up ruins, were held by men, motionless as statues. Colonel Stanton and Sir S. Baker, and other aspiring persons, magnesium wire in hand, were visible perched up on various " coigns of 'vantage." Then flew rockets on high, crossing the Obelisks in their flight, and throwing down on broken towers and walls showers of many-coloured stars. For a time, when this died out, the Temple was left to darkness. But once more, when the party turned into another of the Great Halls, the illumination was renewed. No idea can be given of the effect of the whole device. The Prince and Princess, accustomed to displays of pyrotechnic art, expressed as much pleasure as the other spectators. The moon was at last left to assert its mild supremacy. Seats were placed and carpets spread in one of the Great Halls. We sat there for nearly an hour, amid the twinkle of many small lights, till the Prince and Princess set out to return to the ships. Mrs. Grey mounted a ship of the Desert, and enjoyed a ride on a dromedary; and the Princess, amid a crowd of syces with lanterns, went full canter on her white donkey, at a pace which began to tell on her suite at the last half mile.

Her Royal Highness was so charmed with her ride, that she went back to pick up the part of the cortége in which the Prince was coming at his leisure; and when they arrived at Luxor, they were greeted with ringing cheers, as if to testify the general satisfaction at the brilliant and curious spectacle just witnessed.

CHAPTER X.

LEAVE THEBES.—ESNÉ.—EDFOU.—ASSOUAN.—PHILÆ.

February 19th.—The fleet left Luxor at 5.30, in the light of a lovely dawn. Professor Owen and Mr. Fowler parted company for England last night. It is almost a comfort to hear that the ruins of Erment, which we pass presently, are very ruinous indeed. The temple built by Cleopatra, who is represented on the wall of the chambers, which are all that now remain, has been so much dilapidated that one of our party who visited it, said "it was only little wine cellars, all over hieroglyphics." In a rapid visit, limited in lateral excursions, it is impossible to do justice to Egypt, *i.e.*, to oneself. It is gratifying to find that even Sir Gardner Wilkinson was not able to visit all the places which tradition or ancient remains render worthy of inspection. The fleet arrived at Esné at 12 o'clock. Excellent Mudir of Esné! How great are

the uncertainties of life ! The preparations made to
do honour to the Prince and Princess by this worthy
Governor deserved a better fate than a hasty visit,
while the steamers were coaling and taking in provisions.

Esné was swept, garnished, and whitewashed.
There was a landing-place, with steps, cut from the
river in the soft earth, to an avenue of palm-tree
branches, decorated with standards which scarcely
flew out in the faint breeze. There was a haie
formed from the end of this shady lane by much
be-pistolled Arnaouts and be-scimitared cavasses
to the esplanade, where, in grave ordered line,
stood the white-turbaned sheiks and the masses of
the people in their blue robes, who had strayed
beyond the reach of the muezzin's voice to see the
Royal guests of the Viceroy. Not so much as a
"hush" broke the silence. A better regulated crowd,
in treble line of well-dressed "citizens," could not
well be met in Europe on a similar occasion. Behind
this line of turbaned heads rose the irregular outlines
of the town, with a background of mosque domes,
minarets, and date palms. There was a clear space
of three or four yards spontaneously kept between
the spectators and the banks of the Nile. The
Mudir and his officials were in readiness at the end

of the platform; but, on the receipt of a message from the yacht, they returned to the Governor's house and awaited the Prince's coming in the porch.

I recommend travellers not to neglect paying a visit to the beautiful Temple at Esné, which is worthy of far more notice than Murray gives to it in his admirable Handbook. The wonderful "efflorescence" of the work may, indeed, indicate the advent of the period of decay which came upon Egyptian art and architecture when the Cæsars established their rule in the land, but the richness of the decoration of the vast columns, and the comparatively perfect condition of the remains of this gorgeous Temple of Knuph, entitle it to special attention.

We left Esné soon after 1 o'clock, and maintained a fair speed against the stream. At 4.30 we passed El Kab, where in old times Lucina was worshipped. The Viceroy would not be at all displeased if there were more frequent invocations to the goddess now-a-days, for the population is not increasing, and the great want of the country is people.

Every care was taken to mark our course by flags on the sand-banks, and poles and date branches

in the shallows; the Mudir had men on the look-
out for crocodiles, and did all he could to promote the success of the voyage. But there were

doubts and head-shakings in the land as men
looked on the Nile and thought of the great
steamers, which would have to find their way back.

The heat (78°) was rather trying in the cabins, but on deck, under the awning, it was still fresh.

At dusk we reached Edfou, sixty-two miles above Thebes. Here a party of Ababdeh Arabs, woolly-headed savages, performed a sort of war-dance, and gave an exhibition of sword-play, which was grotesque and ludicrous rather than inspiring or interesting. They embellished it with shrieks and howls like those which, according to poor Aytoun, accompanied the assault of the chief of the clan McTavish on the gallant and lamented Pherson. Hopping on one leg, cutting with a claymore at the adversaries' enormous shield, with crouching to the ground, or leaping in galvanic jumps, was also a feature in this exhibition, for all of which baksheesh was expected.

The woodcut on the preceding page will give a good idea of the Ababdehs.

This evening there occurred the only contretemps —a slight one — of the journey. Shortly before 10 o'clock the Prince of Wales, who was on board the steamer, on deck, observed a light reflected on the side of the dahabeah alongside. He at once gave an alarm. The Princess of Wales and Mrs. Grey were hurried on shore, but the fire was speedily extinguished. The Duke of Sutherland, seizing up a rug, dashed into the cabin, whence the

flames were issuing, and, assisted almost immediately by the Prince and others, beat them down. A
lighted candle in Prince Louis of Battenberg's cabin
had caught one of the curtains. The boat, with all
its muslin and wooden panels and paint, scorched by
an Egyptian sun, not to speak of cartridges and
powder in cases, would have been consumed in a few
minutes, and the explosion might have inflicted considerable damage, and delayed the expedition, had not
the quick eye of the Prince discovered the danger.

February 20th.—(Edfou.) The party landed at
10.30 A.M. and rode over sand and dusty roads to
the Temple, about a mile and a quarter distant. The
Temple, thanks to M. Marriette, is cleared out, and,
thanks to the rubbish which so long saved it from
the destroyer, is in a fair state of preservation. But
the work of destruction is now going on. It is
almost incredible that men can take delight in
chipping away the faces and emblems of the
magnificent work we saw to-day; but those among
us who visited the Temple last year, pointed out
the marks of chisels or stones on the hieroglyphs
and figures which would, if uninjured, make each
massive block an historical record, and render the
Temple a vast volume of knowledge.

Couches and seats were placed in the shade of

the Central Hall, and after the Prince and Princess
had walked through the building, and examined the
emblems which embellish every inch of the walls,
they rested, and the gentlemen had coffee and pipes.
The Royal party returned through the neat, well-
swept, crooked-streeted town. The quiet population
hung carpets out of the windows to do them
honour, and offered curious studies almost from the
nude in real life. At 12.30 the steam-whistle
sounded, the mooring stakes were lifted, and the
flotilla proceeded on its way in all the glory of a
July sun. "What will they say in England"—
the farmers at any rate—when they hear that
the corn is laden with creamy ears, which will be
cut in less than two months, stacked, and garnered,
and that before the Nile rises in June, another crop
—one of maize—will be lifted from the ground?

All went well with us till we came near the
Quarries of Silsilis, about 4.15 o'clock. There the
surface of the stream gave token of the coming
trouble. Soon the Royal yacht stuck hard and
fast. In courtier-like sequence, boat after boat went
soft aground. There was a great deal of " Turn
a heady," " Stope," " Fully speed," " Halfey speed."
Red-fezzed captains danced about emphatically on
the paddle-boxes, and much strong Arabic went

abroad; but the Nile bed would not move, nor
would the ships. The Prince and Princess and all
the company landed on an island sand-bank, as the
sun set behind the Desert ridge. The sailors set
to work to lighten the vessels by carrying the baggage on shore. It needed an hour's hard work and
more—blowing off the water from the boiler, shifting cargo—to float the steamer. When the vessel
forged ahead, there was a general cheer from all
hands. It was near 10 o'clock at night before the
ships were off the bank, and secured to the
mooring-place above Silsilis. The Prince and Princess, Mrs. Grey, Lord Carington, Sir S. Baker,
Prince Louis of Battenberg, came to dinner on
board the Duke of Sutherland's steamer. The
banquet was prepared with great gusto by the
Italian stewards. The Spanish cook gave his most
strenuous efforts to the task, and a masterpiece
of confectionery in burnt almonds, with a flag on
the top inscribed with "Ich Dien," crowned his
triumph. The wind blew strongly, unfortunately,
for the table was laid on the upper deck, and
the candles flared in spite of the awning, and of
artful contrivances of canvas at the sides. It was
the birthday of one of the little Princesses, and
the Duke proposed her health in a neat speech,

and due honour was done to the toast. After dinner, a huge long-legged black sheep, with an enormous pendulous tail, which on the morrow would have been converted into mutton, in a happy moment of inspiration strayed on deck in the way of Lord Stafford, who brought it aft and introduced it to the notice of the Princess. As if it had been accustomed to the best society all its life, the creature, with a tact worthy of a ram-headed "Gentleman in waiting" of the time of the Pharaohs, immediately made itself at home, ate from the Princess's hand, and rose at once to such a height of favour at Court, that its life was spared, by Royal command, and the creature is destined to grow fat and be glad in the pastures of Sandringham. It was decked with a garland of riband when its good future was known, and received many marks of attention in the shape of cabbages and the like from the crew. And now it is "Her Royal Highness's Sheep."

February 21st.—At dawn the flotilla was on its way before the cares of the day had summoned the party to arise. The Nile is so pent in here by the Desert, that the belt of cultivated land can be seen with the naked eye right across on each side; in parts it does not seem to be three miles over. Our great excitement was running aground and getting off again

all day, but there is a permanent, never-failing pleasure in the consciousness of being alive in such a
climate.   Pyramids and ruins have defiled before
us like a panorama, on which we gazed with a
dreamy blissful tranquillity. Nil admirari can be
best understood in Egypt, where there is more
to wonder at than in any land of the earth. Still
it is getting hot—very hot.   There is no denying
it; and it will have been seen, too, that our weather
was not always to be enjoyed.

At 11 o'clock the Prince read prayers in the saloon.
Shortly before 1 o'clock to-day the Royal flotilla
arrived at Assouan, 581 miles south of Cairo.   The
reception was very pretty.   A considerable number
of dahabeahs were moored by the left bank,
on which the town is situated, and the owners
kept up a brisk fusillade in honour of the
occasion, and displayed all their bunting —
British, French, and American.   At the landing-
place there was a stage with coloured lanterns,
lighted up at dusk, and on the flat sandy beach
left by the receding river, was stretched out an
array of caparisoned dromedaries, with horses and
saddled asses, which with their attendants—a crowd
of armed Arnaouts and cavasses—formed an animated foreground to the picture, enclosed by the

fringe of date-palms, and the rocky ridge of the
Desert range beyond. A group of Arabs armed
with shields and long swords, whose hair was
dressed in a fashion that would set the whole
craft of London and Paris at defiance, went through
their exercises, and from a distance was heard the
long wailing cry of welcome which greeted the
passage of the flotilla from all the villages on the
banks as we approached Assouan. An Egyptian
officer in full uniform—French infantry in all but
the fez and sleeve lace—the Mudir, and principal
people of the district, were in waiting; but the day
was hot, and it was arranged that the visit to Philæ,
above the First Cataract, should be deferred till to-
morrow, time being needed to transfer the baggage
and stores to the smaller vessels above. Sir S. Baker
refreshed himself and revived memories of former
travel by a lively tournée or two on a fast dromedary, but did not induce many of the suite to embark on the ships of the Desert. The Prince and
Princess, however, made a short excursion on them,
and paid a visit to the village, which is interesting
to those who care to see where Syene once was.

The news of a little tragedy reached us on shore.
At Edfou we had been told that an Englishman had
shot himself on board his boat, and had been buried

in the Coptic Church. It was not an Englishman,
however, but a young Hungarian noble, Count
Christophe Almàsy. There was only one European
on board with him when the accident occurred, an
Hungarian, whom he picked up at Assouan, and
he avers that the dying man's last words were,
"It was my own fault." He discharged his dragoman at Assouan five days before. The latter
says that the deceased was very careless with his
firearms. Then there are rumours — an actress of
Vienna or Pesth ; but the poor lad lies at rest in
a strange land. He was found lying dead in his
cabin, shot through the body below the breast,
and the direction of the ball in a straight line,
and the situation of the wound, afforded grounds
for suspicion that other hands than his held the
fatal weapon. So dragoman and crew are on their
way to Cairo in irons, to await inquiry.

If Juvenal had spent years composed of such
days as these, he could, perhaps, have borne his
banishment when he thought of sævæ incendia
urbis and the poetæ recitantes in mense Augusto.
But what could he have done in inundation times,
or in the terrible months from June to the end of
September, when the earth is all water and the sky
all fire ? To some of us Assouan was a spot scarcely

less unwelcome than it must have been to the
banished satirist.   The Prince and Princess were
good enough to express a wish that the Duke
and his party should go on with them to the
Second Cataract, but the difficulties—want of boats,
of time, and deficiency of towing power—were not
to be overcome; and it was with great regret we
felt that the desire of our hearts could not be grati-
fied.   Many were the councils and the suggestions
which were held over the matter.   Her Royal Highness would not hear of any obstacle, and announced,
" That it is decided—you are to come on with us."
But, alas! there was the First Cataract—noisy, and
ungentle, and resolute — above us.   Our progress
from Thebes to Assouan, interrupted though it
had been by sand-banks, was delightful; but the
description of a river flowing through a strip of
cultivated land, which is bounded on both sides
by ridges of limestone mountains, and is inha-
bited by the same sort of people, for ever engaged
in the same work, and living in villages as like
each other as two peas, is not apt to prove very
attractive to general readers, even though a Prince
and Princess be en voyage. One date-palm is like
another, each water-wheel is very much the same as
its neighbour, and the shadoofs vary only in the

number of lifts and of the men who work them;
and as to the men — well, unless we go very
close, they are all uncommonly similar in hue and
dress, or want of it, though their rich brown is
now and then diversified by the intense blackness
of the Nubian's epidermis. The halt at sundown,
which allowed every one to go on shore—*i. e.*, the
next field on the bank—was looked for with pleasure, the crowning joy of the day—if it be not
a bull to say so—being the soft cool hours when
the stars twinkled and the moon shone aloft.
Then we were invited to the hospitable saloon of
the Royal yacht, where a gracious welcome awaited
us, and a durbar was held till it was time to walk
the plank, and seek each one his ship by the blazing
torchlights, and sink to sleep, unmolested of mos-
quito, or nightly depredator. But if any one could
have been transported to a reach of the grand old
stream, and could have seen the Royal flotilla, he
would have beheld a spectacle of no ordinary interest. The procession of steamers winding in and
out, ribandwise, and twining along the bends in the
river, with the sun flashing from the white sides and
gilt mouldings of the ships, and reflected back from
the burnished garniture of the saloons, was one of
the prettiest sights possible. The Prince might be

seen standing beneath the awning, on the look-out for birds, with rifle and smooth-bore near at hand, his suite reading or lounging in the easy chairs on deck, and further aft, in a kind of boudoir, all bright with mirrors and golden-backed fauteuils and sofas, one could catch a glimpse of two ladies engaged in reading or sketching. And now all was to end!

February 22nd.—A day of small misadventures for Prince and Princess, and of sorrow pour nous autres. The Nile above Assouan breaks into several streams and meanders through rocky barren islands. It was arranged that Her Royal Highness should proceed by water to the foot of the First Cataract, three miles above Assouan, where donkeys were to be in waiting in charge of Abd-el-Kader, while the Prince went to pay a visit to Lady Duff Gordon, whose dahabeah lay a couple of miles above us. The Princess, attended by the Duke of Sutherland, the Hon. Mrs. Grey, Dr. Minter, Lord Carington, Captain Ellis, and Colonel Marshall, started in a heavy native boat, took a wrong branch of the river, and came to a bank of loose deep sand, on a bed of craggy rocks, under a glaring sun. The Prince, after paying his visit, proceeded to another point below the Cataract, and landed on a place exactly similar, some miles away. Abd-el-

Kader, who had posted far-seeing Arabs on the rocks, was in despair at the news that the Princess's boat was ascending the wrong channel. He dashed round with his corps of donkey-boys, to meet the Princess at the place to which the boat appeared to be going; but when the asses arrived, the Princess was not visible. By some lucky accident, two very wretched donkeys were near the spot where the Princess landed. They had neither saddle nor bridle. On the back of each was a pad without girths, and on these pads the Princess and Mrs. Grey had to poise themselves, and plod towards Philae. The Princess laughed at her novel situation, and appeared to enjoy the newly-found property of balancing herself on a pad, without any girths. The gentlemen of the party were obliged to trudge on foot for three miles over sand into which the foot sank over the ankle at every step, alternating with rocky ridges and scattered stones and boulders. In an hour or so they came up with the Prince and Sir S. Baker, who had waited an hour and a half for their donkeys. The party halted to look at the performance of the Arabs, who swim down the boiling current of the First Cataract in the hope of baksheesh. It has been often described, but it must be seen by those who want to form an idea of savage man as he battles with a mountain torrent, before civilization has washed the energy of his native force out of him. The spectators stand on rocks at the end of the fall, and distance lends decency to the black fellows, who leap in from a ledge one after the other, and in a moment are seen bobbing like the buoys of a fisherman's net, and then, with arms raised aloft alternately, are borne for a quarter of a mile whirling through the whitish foam to the feet of the spectators, and scramble up in their waistcloths to fight for baksheesh. An Arab is never drowned in the rush of waters. Several Englishmen have tried it, and have perished. While the Prince and Princess were continuing their ride towards Philæ, others, who had ridden over direct from Assouan—a route seven miles long over a most trying country, in a sun which would almost have cooked a beefsteak — arrived at the little village below the Island. It does not sound much, but the seven miles were, under the peculiar circumstances, the longest I ever travelled. At the foot, but not under the shade, of two castle-like crags of rock, we found pitched by the bank of the Nile a large tent in three compartments, handsomely carpeted, a dinner-tent capable of receiving forty guests, and

a couple of tents for the accommodation of the
servants. Close at hand were the vessels to which
the Royal party were to be transferred, and long
strings of camels were coming over the Desert with
stores, furniture, and baggage for the voyage to
the Second Cataract. Refreshments had already
been sent to the Island of Philæ, and thither,
heated and thirsty, repaired the weary riders of
stirrupless donkeys from Assouan. A rude bark
ferried us over, and alongside our boat revelled
Naiads, who floated on logs of wood, which they
propelled by foot or hand with great ease, brown
as the wood on which they lay in happy security.
Here is a sketch of one of the water-nymphs of
the Upper Nile and her companion.

We landed on the Sacred Island, which has employed so many pens and pencils in vain. In the blazing sun we wandered about the ruins and prostrate slabs and columns of the Temples. No wonder that visitors came here and ate the priests out of house and home, so that they petitioned Ptolemy to exempt them from the charge of providing them, and had their prayer allowed, as is duly recorded on the walls in Greek—an in terrorem to beggarly travellers. We had no priests to prey upon, and had our own provisions. There are two other inscriptions, which will explain themselves. The first is,—

"L'an VI de la République, le 13 messidor, une armée française, commandée par Bonaparte, est descendue à Alexandrie. L'armée ayant mis, vingt jours après, les Mamelouks en fuite aux Pyramides, Desaix, commandant la première division, les a poursuivis au delà des cataractes, où il est arrivé le 13 ventôse de l'an VII : les généraux de brigade, Davoust, Friant et Belliard ; Donzelot, chef de l'étatmajor ; Latournerie, commandant l'artillerie ; Eppler, chef de la 21ᵉ légère ; le 13 ventôse, an VII de la République, 3 mars, an de J. C. 1799."

The next is,—" R. F. An VII. Balzac, Coquebert, Corabœuf, Costaz, Coutelle, Lacipilère, Ripeault, Lepère, Méchain, Nouet, Lenoir, Nectoux, Saint-

Génis, Vincent, Dutertre, Savigny.—Long. depuis
Paris, 30, 34, 16.   Lat. boréale, 24, 1, 34."

The Royal party came not, and hour after hour
passed away, amid increasing uneasiness, till just
as we had taken boat again, and were returning
to the opposite bank, the shrill cry of joy of the
Nubian women was heard, and a group, among
whom the Prince and Princess, and Mrs. Grey,
were discernible, came in sight, making their way
towards the landing-place, in the rays of the de-
clining sun.   On their return from Philæ, dinner was
served in the large tent, in which a table was laid
out very prettily.   Our cook was in high delight at
being selected to prepare the banquet, but prouder still
was he of the bit of riband, which he fondly believed
to have been worn by the Princess, and put on the
black ram preserved from the knife on Saturday.   As
to the said ram, I regret to report unfavourably.   It
was so pampered the moment it became a favourite
that it became unwell in body and evil in mind.
Raisins, oranges, ratafia, candle-ends, cabbages, and
bonbons are not, it appears, good diet for the sheep
of the Desert.   This, alas! was the farewell banquet.

After dinner, Captain Achmet Hassan proposed
"The Health of the Prince and Princess of Wales,
and of the Duke of Sutherland," in English peculiar

to himself, but his speech was intelligible, and was received as the vivacious officer intended.

The Duke of Sutherland expressed the wishes of his party—"A prosperous voyage and happy return to the Prince and Princess," and proposed, "The Health of the Viceroy," for which Mourad Pasha returned thanks in an excellent speech, in French, giving "The Health of the Queen of England," which was drunk with great enthusiasm by the party upstanding, and with many cheers. By the light of the moon the guests, broken into groups, sat by the river bank, listening to the songs of the Arabs and to the "music" of native performers, till it was time to go, some to the boats, others across the Desert to Assouan, whilst a few resolved to gratify their taste for camping out, by sleeping on the ground, in one of the tents.

February 23rd.—The exertions and fatigues of the previous day infused a certain amount of languor into the movements of the tourists.

The Duke of Sutherland, Lord Stafford, Lord A. L. Gower, and myself, who composed the party designed expressly for the purpose of getting up to see the sun rise, were not so fortunate as we deserved to be, for the sun would insist on rising before we did, and the result was, that only one of the

hardy persons who slept in the tent, roused by
the tremendous war-cry of the Princess's donkey,
awoke; and he, patriarch like, gazed out in solitary
silence on the sand-hills and rocks, warming into
life under the touch of the golden rays which
struck the Desert from the top of the crags beneath
which the tents were pitched.

A wonderful breakfast was spread in the 'large
marquee—fresh fish from the Nile, of strange scale,
said to be good by those who tasted them, and a
succession of dishes very good for the latitude and
longitude. The human vultures came slowly dropping in from Assouan on asses' and camels' backs to
the feast. After breakfast the Princess, notwithstanding the heat, which the absence of any breeze rendered
very trying, was rowed round the Island of Philæ.

There was much to be done in shifting and arranging on board the dahabeahs and the steamer;
and there was a good deal of quiet "looking on"
as the natives conducted the operations.

The Viceroy's French servants and the horses mean-
while were sent on shore, and the baggage reduced
to the smallest compass. But still the Royal boats
were full enough, and Arabs, Egyptian sailors,
boxes of provisions, coops of fowl and turkeys, and
live-stock, lumbered the decks.

T

In the dahabeah with the Prince and Princess were Mrs. Grey and Prince Louis of Battenberg; in the second boat Colonel Teesdale, Lord Carington, Sir S. Baker, Mourad Pasha, Mr. Montagu, Captain Ellis, Dr. Minter, and Mr. Brierly; and beds for two were laid on deck under an awning, as the accommodation was limited. A third boat, laden with coal and provisions, was towed by the small steamer in which the Royal domestics and attendants were embarked, and in which the cooking was carried on. It was past 3 o'clock before all the preparations for the upward voyage were complete.

Long time loth to depart, we halted on the bank; but at last the hour came for the Royal party, in diminished state, to start on their course to the Second Cataract. The Prince and Princess received the Duke of Sutherland and his friends, and Colonel Stanton, Major Alison, and Sir H. Pelly, who were returning to Thebes, on board, and with many sincere expressions of respect, and hearty wishes for their prosperous journey and happiness, we bade their Royal Highnesses good-bye, and returned to Assouan, in order to descend the Nile to Cairo. To use the words of a little diary I have seen, " We were all very sorry to part company."

CHAPTER XI.

"I do perceive here a divided duty." I am in what would in familiar speech be termed "a fix." The Prince and Princess have, to our infinite regret, separated from the party with which I am travelling, and are bound up the river, which we are about to descend. The Duke and his friends are setting out for home in a few days after their arrival in the Egyptian capital. It is plain that I can no longer write from my own knowledge of what occurs as the Royal travellers stem the stream. They are in the hands, so to speak, of Sir Samuel Baker, who does not pretend to any acquaintance with this Lower Nile, and whose Arabic, as he approaches the regions in which he learned his pronunciation of the language, comes into play. Whilst they are away, I must pass the time as best I can, for the Prince was good enough to desire, as I had no

T 2

pressing engagements compelling me to return to
England with my party, that I would meet or
await him at Cairo. Assouan has no abiding place.
At Thebes, indeed, I might halt for a while, as
Colonel Stanton is to stay at Luxor, on his way
down, in order to dig for antiquarian treasures in
hallowed ground sasigned to the Prince.* But
success is doubtful, and as it is, his steamer does
not contain much extra accommodation. Then how
hard it would be to part with those who have been
my companions for many miles and hours, and who
have made them pass so pleasantly away! I am
compelled to ask my readers to leave the Royal
party for a while, and to come with us down the
Nile, share an excursion to Jerusalem, revisit the
Suez Canal, and so return to Cairo, where they
will find the Prince and Princess, with whom we
will travel together till their wanderings in the
East are brought to a close.

On our way back from Philæ to Assouan, the
Duke and some of his party paid a visit to Lady
Duff Gordon, whose "Letters" on Egypt had proved
so interesting on our voyage. The Prince's visit

---

* It is a way the Viceroy has of according favours to his friends.
Thus Lord Dufferin has a digging of which he granted the usufruct to
the Duke in case he was inclined to prosecute researches.

caused her very great pleasure and cheered her exceedingly. Her son had been down to the flotilla several times, and gave but sorry accounts of her health—the sad cause of her exile for so many years from home and family. At any moment her life, hanging on a slender thread, might cease. The warmth of her nature has been touched by the apparent degradation of the Egyptian people, and in her letters she has written of the Government, and especially of Ismail Pasha, with great severity. Her physical weakness rendered her dependent on others, and there is no doubt that, perceiving the direction of her mind and the tendency of her inquiries, those around her were disposed to exaggerate any acts which seemed repressive or harsh, and to find out causes of complaint. Some time ago Lady Gordon resided in rickety rooms, constructed of very frail materials, in a story of a ruined temple at Luxor; but now she lives in a dahabeah, which is at present moored above the town of Assouan, in a sort of pool a couple of miles below the Falls or Cataract. Most travellers call on the invalid, and find it worth their while, if they are received, for her conversation is spirituel and animated, and she has a great deal of information, rather about the people, however, than the country. We found our Mr. Duff Gordon on board the boat, which was in the full blaze of the sun, but was covered in on deck; a modest but not uncomfortable dahabeah, with a group of natives on deck, among whom we recognized Lady Gordon's often-quoted dragoman without the need of any description.

The lady was reclining on a sofa in the cabin, which was cool and airy. Her face, notwithstanding traces of severe illness, presented in its fine outlines a type of distinction and refinement, and her clear deep eyes looked out on the world with an expression full of sincerity and enthusiasm. But her features were worn, and the hectic on her cheek, the colour of her lips, and her wasted hands and frame, prepared one for the difficulty with which she spoke, and for the cough and catching of the breath which interrupted her conversation. She wore a long, loose, oriental robe, and a fez cap, beneath which appeared her hair, fast turning white, cut short all round. At this time there is an unusual trouble upon the poor lady. A French newspaper, seizing on a passage in one of her letters written long ago, in which she described the misery of the fellaheen and rated the Viceroy very sharply, has a bitter article on the reported engagements of Mdlle. Schneider and other expensive artists for the Cairo Theatre. Ismail Pasha has been made aware of the attack, and is said to be much incensed against the writer. Indeed, Lady Duff Gordon believes that she is scarcely safe, poor lady, and is sure that Omar, her dragoman, will fall on evil days when she is no more. I find that the most—as they seem to me—extravagant notions prevail respecting the Government at Cairo. Poisoning, strangling, drowning, are said to be common modes of getting rid of obnoxious persons. But in one case given by Lady Gordon, of a wealthy native gentleman exiled for some slight offence to certain death in Fezegoloo, it was stated to us that the man was alive and well on his estates on good English authority. Lady Gordon led the conversation to the condition of the Egyptian peasantry, and was giving an account of the apathy of the Viceroy in the presence of the famine in Upper Egypt now imminent, when Omar, who came in with pipes and coffee, interposed, and said that so many thousand measures of corn had just been sent up for the people. Perhaps this information might not have been forthcoming had we not been present. Our visit lasted only half an hour, as we were obliged to get on board our steamer and prepare for the return voyage.*

When we got back to Assouan, a telegraphic despatch from Lord Clarendon was awaiting the

---

* Since the above lines were written, intelligence has reached England of the death of Lady Duff Gordon.

Consul-General, to be forwarded to the Prince, which was sent off by dromedary about 5 o'clock, and which the Prince received next day.

The telegraph wires are stretched (with the exception of one break in the Desert) away to distant Dongola. The posts are visible as we follow the course of the river, on the banks of which plod the reluctant camel and the patient peasantry. Pharaoh is bent on swift intercourse with all parts of his far-reaching viceroyalty. The water-wheel in use thousands of years ago works creakingly by the side of the stream, along which stretch the silent wires. Before the smoke of the little fleet has been lost to the view of the half-scared labourers who stare at the pageant, Cairo knows how the guests of the Viceroy are speeding and faring on their way, as his steamers stem the current towards that mystic South, where, hid in the mountains of an unknown continent, lie the sources of the great river which has been a wonder through all the centuries that man can count in his history.

Cook's tourists have also arrived! Their steamers are just below us in the stream. The tourists are all over the place. Some are bathing off the banks; others, with eccentric head-dresses, are toiling through the deep sand, after an abortive attempt to reach Philæ.

They are just beaten by a head in the race! Another day, and the Prince and Princess would have been at their mercy. It is whispered that various unexpected causes of delay occurred down the river—that coal was short; that supplies of provisions failed at certain places; that the steamers went aground very often. At all events, the tourists were just too late, and they return to-morrow, disconsolate.

Wednesday, February 24th.—When we got up this morning, our steamer was many miles north of Assouan, which we left at daybreak. She floundered, now aground, now afloat, over the shoals at Silsilis—the narrowest part of the river, by the bye—followed by the Consul's steamer; and in the evening she reached Esné, ninety-two miles, and moored for the night. There was nothing to be done all day but take long shots at birds on the banks with rifles. Once a deadly tube was levelled at what was pronounced to be a crocodile. In another instant, who knows what would have happened?—for just as the finger was tightening on the trigger, a man made out with a glass the object to be an Arab rolled up in his cloak asleep on the sand! Every one says we ought to have stopped for an hour at Silsilis, where there are most interesting remains, and very ancient and renowned quarries. Every one asks why we did not stop, and no one answers the question.

February 25th.—A hot wind. Ran down from Esné rapidly, and reached Thebes (Luxor) at breakfast-time (thirty-two miles). Went on shore; called on Mustapha Aga, who made presents of scarabs all round. Wandered over the place all day, and made a most delightful excursion, in the bright moonlight, to Karnak, where we mounted up to the top of a gigantic pylon, and sat watching the stars, and talking mild philosophy, far into the night. I am not sure that the ruins were not more impressive in their silent vastness, with the moonbeams resting on the broken walls, and casting mysterious shadows across the mighty halls, than they were when touched up with red, blue, and green—nay, I am sure they were. Perched up here, one can almost agree with Hekekyan Bey, that the eye of the ancient priest was a better astronomical instrument than a six-foot achromatic, that is, under the conditions he specified. " With his senses purified by fasting, and his mind cleared by vigil, the Pharaohonic astronomer, coming out of a dark chamber in the heart of the pyramid and taking his lonely stand on the level ledge, could observe the motions of the heavenly bodies, and detect their actions, at least as well as the modern philosopher, who has been eating rich meats and drinking wines, although he may have fine optical instruments to aid him." The quantity of wine would certainly have something to do with the matter.

February 26th.—It was after 6 o'clock when our steamer, towing a felucca, in which the Princess's sheep was a forecastle passenger, left Luxor, lighted equally by sun and moon. Colonel Stanton remained at Thebes, with Sir Henry Pelly and Major Alison to assist in his explorations. Mustapha Aga was not visible, but Said, his son, bound on occult errands, took a passage with us. We reached Keneh at 11 o'clock. The Consular Agent's son came on board, and invited us to a banquet in the town. It would be interesting to ascertain what idea our Consular person at Keneh has of the empire he represents. The representative of Said Hamed Omazeen received the translation of the Duke's speech refusing the invitation, and explaining that we were making for Cairo with all speed, with obvious disappointment.

As some consolation, the Duke and party wrote their names on a sheet of note-paper, which gave him every satisfaction. There was at all events no need of imitating the caution of Talleyrand on a similar occasion.   Here Said of Luxor left us, and was seen glorious on a donkey, vanishing like a shadow, desertwards, followed by another animal of the same kind laden with his bed.   Oh! Said, where is my ——— No! perhaps you forget all about it, and I will not jog your memory.   Whilst the steamer was coaling, great excitement was extracted out of the accidental appearance of an empty bottle in the river.   At the sight some mud-coloured Egyptians, who had been sitting in a boat near at hand, silent and motionless as so many Sphinges, bounded into life, threw off their simple garments, and dashed into the flood.   They are strong swimmers, these Arabs.   They swim edgeways, throwing aloft their arms alternately, and dragging them through the water so that the head and shoulders rise out of the stream, as they strike powerfully down with their legs.   The empty bottle bobbed up and down in the current, and one fine young fellah, running through his horses, seized it, and returned triumphantly to shore.   The fun was not allowed to slacken for want of material.   The Nile bristled with empty bottles, and the water was alive with black shaven heads, belonging to vigorous bodies and contending arms.   One master executed a feat; caught two bottles in one hand, held a

third in the other, and pushed a fourth before him
with his chest. The hand with the two bottles was
held aloft, the other he used to keep his course, and
thus, after performing a tour de force in the water
which it would puzzle many a champion swimmer
at home to accomplish in such a stream, he gained
the edge of the boat from which he leaped.

Soon after leaving Kench, the steamer alighted on
a sand-bank, and Ali Captan sacrificed several of the
crew to his divine rage at the water being so low, or
the land being so high, and abused all the natives
visible on shore in very effective Arabic. In vain
the crew poled in the way in vogue in Thames
steamers when they got aground about Kew, or
Hampton Court. In vain boats filled with chocolate-
coloured fellahs, who leaped into the water neck
high, and shoved with all their force—little it must
have been in such a case, as they could scarcely keep
their legs—came off from shore in quick succession ;
it was only by putting out an anchor, and working
on it with hawsers, that we backed off the steamer,
after an hour's hard work. In an hour more the
vessel stuck again. Once more there came from
shore a swarm of fellahs, who grunted like a marsh
full of frogs, their heads alone above the flood ,
muscular fellows, with square high shoulders and

narrow hips, the type of the ancient race depicted in
the temples; light and thin, but, as a rule, fairly
grown and well made. They feed on the coarsest
bread, pulses, and maize. Their sole drink is water.
Not one had bad or discoloured teeth. When a boat
alongside, which F. M. and myself strove to keep
from crushing them, by fending off from the saloon
windows, swerved in, they were obliged to crouch
down up to their noses. Some of the shorter went
quite under, and, cork-like, bobbed up again. Although the sun was hot, they shivered, with chattering teeth, as if it were mid-winter. At 6 o'clock
the ship was put round, and made fast to the left
bank, at Reiseah, a very poor village, surrounded as
usual by date and doum trees. This grounding cost
us two whole hours, and our craft gave signs of rough
usage in extra creaking and shaking. It was full
moon, and after dinner some of us strolled on shore,
and had an opportunity of inspecting the working of
the police system, which is really as perfect as that
of London—in some respects, at all events. If dogs
will bark at roving Englishmen, roving Englishmen
will pelt dogs. A yelping of many dog power, caused
by the overthrow of a huge cur by a well aimed
brickbat, eliminated from some shaded retreat a
native gentleman, armed with a sharp short spear,

who "invited" the truants to return to their ship
in vain. He sent off a comrade, who returned with
an ancient firelock, and his feelings " may be more
readily imagined than described" when he saw the
illustrious strangers turning their faces towards the
river and yielding to timid solicitations, which
indeed they did not need, as the dogs had all fled.

Having achieved this victory, the man of the spear

and the man of the firelock sat down on the bank by
our watch-fire, and awaited events. It so happened

that there was a great one to wind up our night. Between the Italian intendance and the Egyptian crew, from Captain to lamp-lighter, there was a great gulf fixed, in which raged a sea of acrimony and distrust. From time to time wine had been missed on board, and suspicion, like an agitated sparrow, flew from place to place, and rested on head after head. Now, however, for an anonymous person, employed to act as an animated lighthouse on shore when the steamer moored for the night, hitherto in moderate repute, some malignant star rose. He was caught by Giovanni's brother gliding away with two bottles of our finest Sauterne. Terentio, joyous, came swift to the saloon, and advised Ali Risa of the fact. That much-besought-after officer laid aside his cigar, hastened on deck, held court, and pronounced sentence. Oh, Allah! How the silent night was rendered hideous by the edict of that righteous and not over stern judge! As Anonymous had offended on former occasions by staring at the Prince and Princess—as moreover there was reason to think he was the committer of many a previous larceny — the sentence was that he be then and there put over the side, and allowed to find his way to Cairo as well as he could. His worldly goods consisted of a piece of sackcloth, a bottle, and a ragged calico gown, and these were

handed over the gangway readily. But their owner
was a stout fellow, and desperate. His shouts were
fiendish; he resisted fiercely the efforts of four men
to eject him, till with a shove all together he
was sent bounding on shore, where the policemen and
a sheik seated by the watch-fire were the only
spectators of his calamity. How he screamed and
yelled, and invoked the moon to hear him! How
he called on the Duke to protect him, and cited a
long life of unblemished reputation and the names
of famous ancestors as proofs of his innocence! He
danced on the beach, kicked out the watch-fire,
and for more than an hour kept shouting and
appealing to Ali Risa. At last the latter lost all
patience, called to sheik and policemen, and the de-
linquent was swiftly carried away into the interior, in
a tempest of outcries which was worthy of an angry
menagerie. Spirits of mischief were on the wing. As
we were sitting quietly in the cabin shortly after this,
bang went a gun in the village. After a minute the
report of a musket was heard from the opposite shore
—then another; and so in a moment of enthusiasm
I took out a Colt, which had been loaded the day
before the first unlucky Battle of Bull Run, and discharged barrel after barrel towards the opposite shore,
silencing the enemy's fire, and extorting the admira-

tion of the sheik and policemen. What the firing
was about no one could divine, but more than one
heard the singing of a bullet. It is probable the
shots were fired by village watchmen to show they
were on the alert. There are robbers on the river,
and there is perturbation concerning a Greco-Italian
who is missing. He was apparently of a trustful or
ostentatious character, for he showed gold and silver,
to be observed of men in all places. Setting out
from Sioot on a mule of well-known perversity, he
was entreated by the Governor not to proceed, but he
was as obstinate as the animal itself. Well, the mule
never pulled up till it reached a station fourteen hours
from Sioot, where hunger induced the quadruped to
halt the next morning. The sheik of the town
begged the traveller to change mules. But he would
not: he mounted once more, and he may be making
straight for the Mountains of the Moon, for man or
mule have not been heard of since, and anxious
inquiries have been already made after him by the
Government, acted on by the consul, from Cairo.

Saturday, February 27th.—We left Reiseah, the
City of the Outcast, rather too long after daybreak. Our captain, for an Egyptian, is not very
matinal, and such a shock as he had to his
nervous system last night is not easily recovered.

There is a perceptible coldness in the air when
the sleeping-cabin window is opened by the early
riser; he is more apt to feel a sharp wind than he
was a week ago. We are running against the ever-
blowing north breeze, instead of going with it.
Last night the air was so chilly I was glad to
gather up the discarded quilted cotton bed-cover,
and draw it over the blankets. In council last night
it was decided to stop at Girgeh, in order to visit
the temples and ruins at Abydus; but when the
morning broke a change fell upon us. The day
turned out to be an abominable anachronism — a
dim, watery sky, a wind driving sand and dust,
and not a ray of accustomed sunshine. Belianeh
is the proper place to land if the traveller desires
to go to Abydus; but Ali Risa stated that no
donkeys could be procured there, as we had made
no previous arrangements for the purpose, and that
we must go on to Girgeh. So speeding on, men
became vacuous as to Abydus. Murray was fur-
tively looked at and laid aside. It could not be
said he gave the least encouragement to any one
desirous of shirking Abydus on the ground that
it was destitute of interest. Hamed was consulted:
he declared roundly that it took two hours and a
half to go to Abydus on the very best donkeys, and

that a fair average was three hours—then an hour at
least would be needed for the most hasty survey
of the ruins, so that it would be dark ere we could
get back to Girgeh, and then it would be too late
to move that night. Need I say what the result
was? At 10.40 A.M. The Ornament of the Two
Seas swept past Girgeh in triumph. No doubt
most of us flattered ourselves that in a good time
coming we shall visit Abydus with a favouring
wind and no dust.

The skipper relieved the monotony of the course
by occasionally arranging attachments between the
bottom of the ship and the bed of the Nile, and,
rightly or wrongly, came in for a good deal of the
censure which is like to be sent forth from travellers
vexed with flies and idleness. Mem. as to flies—
a veil with large net, or a piece of coarse gauze,
stretched over a sheet of pasteboard, with a hole
cut in it to fit the head, is a very good fly-
phylactic—I invented it in India, and used it
with marked success. You can breathe, read, and
write with your head-dress on, and if you wear
gloves you will be quite able to set at defiance the
loathsome, fat, filthy, persecuting plagues, and enjoy
their mortification even though you be laughed at
for your strange guise.

At Souhadj, where the steamer halted for nearly an hour to take in coal, there was a repetition of the scenes so familiar at every town along the banks of the Nile. The same women busy drawing water, washing feet and legs, crouching on the sand, or stalking away, with water-jars on their heads, like stately animals going to their lairs— the same children along the banks—the same men, in blue gowns and white turbans, squatted in the same sized coteries. Ali Risa went on shore and took up with the same manner of sheiks as he met before. Collections of mudirs, scribes, and cavasses were at hand to welcome him, as if they had all hurried on from the last station. The same old men and boys, in tattered clothes, came on board with the same small bags full of coal, and emptied them into the bunkers; and as for houses, date-trees, and pigeon colonies and buzzards, it would be hard to say in what they differed from those seen anywhere else in our course up and down. Souhadj is a city of great importance, and promises, if not washed away by the Nile, to become greater. At the spot where the steamer was fastened, there were one doctor and two sheiks, three sheep, two donkeys, saddled, one buffalo calf, three black boys, three women with veiled heads, a dim-eyed, toothless hadjee of great size, smoking a short chibouque, and seven fellahs, all packed on top of water-jars and bags of merchandise in a small craft, sunk down to the mud-plastered gunwales. The buffalo mother, with a rope fastened round her nostrils, in charge of a lad on shore, stared, with that peculiar wild look which marks the animal, at her disconsolate calf; but she was not to be separated, for the lad swam off with the end of the rope, which was made fast to the side, and then, as the sail was loosed, the poor creature was dragged along, struggling and blowing, and half-drowning in the water, till her struggles threatened to overturn the boat, and she was cast off to return to shore, where she stood, piteously calling to her young one, till she was butted on board a larger boat to join it at the other side. Another skiff crammed full of shrouded women, turbaned men, asses, goats, sheep, a horse, general merchandise, and children was also bound to the other bank of the river, because the administration was supposed to be less severe. Migration is much in favour still in Egypt. Half a village will vanish in a night, with a celerity and completeness to be envied by the less expert practitioners in more civilized lands.

The Governor, poor man! was in much distress at
the receipt of an order to send 2,000 turkeys to
Cairo for the purpose of assisting at feasts to be
given on the occasion of the marriage of one of the
Viceroy's daughters. But that is not all. If our
interpreters were not wrong in gathering up and
rendering the rumours which perplexed the councils
of Souhadj, a similar order had been sent to each
of the eight governors of provinces; so that an
army of 16,000 turkeys is demanded by the agents
of the Viceroy. The fellahs are driven into a market
which has, of course, followed the usual law of
supply and demand. They pay 100 piastres for
a turkey, and they get only 20 or 25 piastres
from the Government.

We left Souhadj with every wish for the success
of the worthy Governor in bagging his birds, and
delved through the river under great crags, perforated
with mummy caves, which rise above the eastern
bank. When Ali Captan was minded to run in shore
at sundown, for the night, the suppressed energies
of certain among us were aroused, and he was forced
to go on for a place marked Teme in Leake's map.
It is not easy to imagine what satisfaction is caused
by a little triumph of this sort over surrounding
functionaries, or the proportionate prostration of the

official mind at · being thwarted in the selection of
time and place for the conclusion of the day. A
lazy man, who wished to gain a reputation for active
habits, caused some resentment by objecting to the
compulsory proceeding on the ground that he would
have liked to have gone on shore for half an hour to
take a walk before dark; which hypothetical peram-
bulation he insinuated he would have indulged in
had the Captain been allowed to take up his quarters
at an earlier hour.

At night the wind fell—it would appear to be its
wont at this time of year in the evening—and the
moon, after a conflict with a screen of encumbering
clouds, cast them off, and sailed forth into a blue
clear sea of sky; a small moon, however, neither
so bright nor so large as we see her in less genial
lands, nearer the cold and vaporous North.

www.ingramcontent.com/pod-product-compliance
Lightning Source LLC
Chambersburg PA
CBHW020952030726